DON'T BE TAKEN FOR AN EXPENSIVE RIDE.

HENRY P. COSTANTINO

First Edition

TRANSPORTATION PUBLISHING COMPANY

MISSION VIEJO, CALIFORNIA

TM

MOVING?
DON'T BE TAKEN FOR AN EXPENSIVE RIDE.

By Henry P. Costantino

Copyright © 1988 by Henry P. Costantino

Printed in the United States of America

Library of Congress Cataloging-in-Publication Data

Costantino, Henry P., 1947-
    Moving? : don't be taken for an expensive ride.

    1. Storage and moving trade--United States--
Handbooks, manuals, etc. 2. Moving, Household--
United States--Handbooks, manuals, etc. I. Title.
HE5623.C673 1988   648'.9   87-9182
ISBN 0-945155-03-4 (pbk.)

This book is available to businesses and organizations at quantity discounts, when used for sales promotion, business, or educational purposes. For information, contact:
Transportation Publishing Co., Volume Sales Dept.,
P.O. Box 2309-B, Mission Viejo, CA 92690

PUBLISHER'S GUARANTEE

After reading this book, if you are unable to obtain a discount when using a professional moving company on your relocation to another state, you can receive a refund for the full purchase price of this book.

To receive your refund, just return the book with a copy of your proof of purchase and a copy of the final bill (Bill of Lading) received from the moving company, that shows the exact amount paid for your move. By comparing the prices with those in the company rate book, one can easily determine if discounts were given.

IMPORTANT

MOVING? DON'T BE TAKEN FOR AN EXPENSIVE RIDE is designed to provide information in regard to the subject matter covered. It is sold with the understanding that the publisher and author are not engaged in rendering legal, accounting or other professional services. If legal or other expert assistance is required, the services of a competent professional should be sought.

The suggestions given are the opinion of the author only. Every effort has been made to make this book as complete and as accurate as possible. However, there may be mistakes both typographical and in content. All prices and regulations stated herein can vary from company to company, county to county, and day to day. Furthermore, information herein is current only to the date of publishing. Therefore, this information should be used only as a guide.

The purpose of this book is to educate and entertain. The author and publisher shall not accept liability or responsibility to any person or entity with respect to any loss or damage caused directly or indirectly by information contained in this book.

To Tony, Bertha, and Jan - for incessant
support and encouragement ...

Edited by Mary Tilton
Cover illustration by Richard Montoya
Text illustrations by Bernie Custodio

TABLE OF CONTENTS

SECTION 1
WHAT IS IT ALL ABOUT?   15
- general background (a deregulated industry)
- determining transportation costs
  (how the professionals do it)
- the "bad news phone call"
  (no longer necessary)
- the estimate, plus 10% rule
  (still in effect today)

SECTION 2
THE NEW GAME IN TOWN!   21
- no longer a need for surprises
  (getting written guarantees)
- what deregulation of the industry
  means to your pocketbook/wallet

SECTION 3
SELECTING THE "RIGHT COMPANY"   25
- how to minimize mistakes
  (avoid becoming a "bad news" statistic)
- what Mr. Smart might do
  (learn how an experienced person does it)
- utilizing the process of elimination
  (the selection process)
- list of companies which presently
  guarantee prices
- the network system of agents
  (don't take anything for granted)

.

THE STRUCTURE OF THIS BOOK

MOVING? DON'T BE TAKEN FOR AN EXPENSIVE RIDE
has two distinct parts.

Sections 1 through 6 include most everything you need to know when selecting a professional moving company: brief background about pricing within the industry; how to obtain a binding (guaranteed) estimate; how to select the "right company"; what services are available and what prices to expect; what can and cannot be negotiated; how to negotiate the most reasonable price for services requested; what "extras" are available; how to properly schedule dates for loading and unloading; how weekend loading/unloading overtime charges sometimes can be avoided; how to receive $100 to $125 per day for each day the company is late picking up or delivering your possessions, and much more. Section 4, "What To Expect From The Professionals" is the most vital section in the book.

The second half of this book (Sections 7-13) includes other helpful information, advice and tips to make a professional relocation safe and economical; special circumstances that may develop; how to save money using the Post Office and other alternatives; what to move and what to discard; packing tips for the do-it-yourselfer; what to do if your new home is not ready for occupancy; how you may be able to write off the cost at tax time; how to transport plants, pets and automobiles; helpful tips on organizing the entire procedure; common questions and answers with a host of other useful "golden nuggets of knowledge".

Throughout the book there are helpful photos and illustrations to guide you through the entire process. Also, little splashes of humor have been included. In a stressful situation, humor does have some degree of therapeutic, tension-releasing ability. Even for a "veteran mover", anxiety and tension are unavoidable facts of life.

The publisher welcomes comments concerning personal experiences. Of particular interest would be the total estimate of money that was saved. Comments will be placed in a separate section, in the next edition of this book. Therefore, please state whether or not permission is granted to use your name when quoting from comments. Forward all correspondence to Transportation Publishing Company (address is on copyright page).

INTRODUCTION

Deregulation was instituted to help consumers obtain a variety of new services, at reasonable prices. It certainly has accomplished that goal within the interstate transportation industry. The problem with this industry has been one of consumer awareness. People have simply not been adequately informed as to how they can benefit!

Since Congress deregulated other industries such as banking, air transportation and long distance telephone service, consumers have benefited from the fierce competition for their dollars. The airline industry has been forced to lower prices while absorbing the cost for huge advertisements in newspapers and magazines throughout the country. Costly television and radio commercials also have been used to get the message to the consumer. Banking and long distance telephone service companies have followed a similar course. They increased their advertising budgets significantly, in order to compete for their share of the market.

All three of these deregulated industries have been forced into informing and advising consumers how they can save money, earn more money or receive better service. They are doing a tremendous job of explaining how deregulation has resulted in a variety of new services, as well as lower costs to those who utilize each service. Our free enterprise system has encouraged them to provide this information. Competition has always been a strong motivator!

When was the last time you saw an advertisement on television or in a newspaper, explaining how the consumer has benefited since Congress passed the Motor Carrier Act of 1980?

Since that time, millions of people have moved from one state to another. However, few people know how they could have saved money, or can presently save money on interstate relocations, while using the services of a professional moving company. A smaller number of people know the wide range of new and improved services that are available.

Occasionally, an isolated article may appear in a magazine or local newspaper explaining a particular service being offered. Maybe you will find a few helpful tips which were specifically written for the "do-it-yourselfer". Many of the articles and previous books written on this subject have been compiled by individuals who never worked in the industry. They have been professional writers, interior designers, or people with a limited amount of experience who wish to convey their knowledge of the industry. While their intent has been honorable, the information has been somewhat sketchy and incomplete. Many of the facts are peppered with misconceptions that are no longer applicable or relevant in today's marketplace.

Knowledge is the key to a safe, economical and hassle-free relocation. There are numerous ways to approach all of the little details which need to be addressed. The reader will learn how to avoid becoming a "bad news" statistic! By following the step-by-step instructions, the reader can minimize the cost while receiving quality service. It is possible for an informed customer to save a significant amount of money.

The author has heard many "horror stories". Most could have been avoided if people knew what questions to ask, and the variety of alternatives available. If they knew what was reasonable to request, they probably would have achieved better results. Those important and reasonable questions will be thoroughly answered.

The Interstate Commerce Commission has never encouraged moving companies to use the word "discount". However, it does allow them to "negotiate" under certain conditions. Cost for transportation, boxes and labor for packing of boxes supplied by the company are typical examples. Learning how to negotiate is important in order to get the most cost-effective move.

Because of deregulation, not all companies charge the same amount or offer the same services. Prices and services may be similar, but not always the same. There are also many options which differ between companies.

Each company must receive approval from the I.C.C. for whatever it wishes to offer. Usually, if one company decides to provide a new service, most of the other larger companies try to offer the same service shortly thereafter. Today, there is a wide range of services to choose from with each company offering its own version. The consumer can no longer assume that all companies are the same. Since 1980, those days are gone!

In the past, a few companies have received "bad press" on national television and in other news media, because of abuses by a few irresponsible or dishonest individuals in the industry. In recent years, the I.C.C. has worked closely with interstate moving companies to establish safeguards which protect the consumer. Irregularities and abuses are no longer commonplace. Regulations and procedures have been tightened to provide more protection for the public.

Throughout the entire book, the author assumes the role of "devil's advocate". This gives the reader an opportunity to learn the secrets of getting a cost-effective relocation from an experienced moving consultant/salesman "inside the industry". Detailed information is included which is up-to-date and easy to read.

SECTION 1

WHAT IS IT ALL ABOUT?

"... and the times they are a changing."
-Bob Dylan

Every year, millions of families and individuals move from one state to another. Unfortunately, not all of them move as cheaply as they might. There have been many books and scattered articles written about relocating. However, there is very little information available which reveals the money-saving secrets of moving with a professional company.

Hiring the professionals to perform this grueling task may not be as costly as you think. In fact, it may not cost too much more than doing it yourself. Obviously, it will cost more, but you can narrow the margin considerably.

Consumers can financially benefit from the deregulation of the moving industry which was passed by Congress in 1980. However, they need to learn how to shop for the "right company". They must know what questions to ask, what services are available, and what the alternatives are.

The purpose of this book is not to teach everything there is to know about the moving and storage industry. What will be learned is a step-by-step approach to saving money, while still

15

receiving quality services. Follow the advice and methods closely, from beginning to end. They will save you lots of hard-earned money. If you are fortunate to have your employer paying for the relocation, you can bet the company will be happy you took the time to reduce its corporate expenditures.

If moving companies in your community are still using transportation prices approved by the Interstate Commerce Commission, they probably will not continue to do so for much longer. The I.C.C. provides an opportunity to reduce rates under certain conditions. In most communities, an educated consumer can usually obtain reduced rates. Competition in this multi-billion dollar industry has been fierce since it has been deregulated. Every company is fighting for your business. You will learn that price differences can sometimes be enormous between companies.

Most people do not know the interstate transportation industry has been deregulated. Most importantly, if they are aware of this fact, they do not know how to benefit, in dollars and cents, as a result.

Before explaining how to save money while getting the price guaranteed, it is important to know how pricing was established prior to deregulation. This segment is not being included to bore you to death. It is essential that you understand the basics! When the time comes to intelligently negotiate with the professionals, you should know almost as much about pricing as the company representative who comes to your residence.

If you moved prior to deregulation, the procedure followed something like this: You called a moving company to ask what it would cost to move to your new home in another state. The company obliged by mailing its literature immediately. A few days later, you received a colorful brochure stressing its safety record and integrity - but not mentioning price. If time allowed, maybe two or three companies were contacted.

After reading the fancy brochures, you followed the instructions to call for more information. It was suggested a salesperson visit your home to provide a cost estimate.

16

A few days later, a representative arrived. He or she toured your home with a clipboard, making notations on an inventory sheet. When the inventory was completed, the estimator determined the total weight of your household goods. After leafing through a few pages in the I.C.C. tariff book (book of rates), the estimator arrived at an estimate of cost. The "rate" for transportation was listed in dollars and cents for each 100 pounds being transported so many miles.

Before deregulation, a driver performing an interstate move was required to weigh the van before going to the residence. Once the household goods were loaded on the truck, the driver would return to a scale and weigh the truck a second time. The difference in the two weighing procedures would determine the actual total poundage of your household.

EXAMPLE (use only as a guideline, since rates are fictitious)

Miles	1000-1999 Lbs	2000-3999 Lbs	4000-7999 Lbs	8000-11999 Lbs
201-220	$45	$34	$28	$24
221-240	$46	$35	$29	$25
241-260	$47	$36	$30	$26
261-280	$48	$37	* $31	*$27
281-300	$49	$38	$32	$28

Using the fictitious rates in the preceding chart as an example, if there were 4500 pounds of household goods to be moved 265 miles, the rate for each 100 pounds would be $31. Therefore, the basic transportation cost would be $31x45 ($1395 total). As you would expect, the transportation rate rises as the amount of miles needed to transport the shipment increases. However, you also will notice the rate for each 100 pounds decreases as the size of the load increases.

To transport an 8000-pound shipment the same amount of miles as the 4500-pound household, the rate shown is $27 for each 100 pounds. You should keep in mind that it has never been cheaper to move a larger shipment, only less money for each 100 pounds being moved the same amount of miles. Even though the price for each 100 pounds goes down as the load gets significantly larger, you then must multiply that rate times a larger number. In the example, $27 would be multiplied by 80 for an 8000-pound shipment being moved 265 miles, $27x80 = ($2160 total). The household that weighed 4500 pounds only costs $1395 for the basic transportation cost.

This used to be the only way to compute the actual cost for transportation. All moving companies used the same tariff book. Every company that surveyed a residence would have arrived at the same total dollar amount, providing the estimator calculated the same total poundage. If one company figured a lower transportation cost, it was only because a lower poundage figure was estimated by the representative. Nobody knew for sure what the actual cost would be until the entire shipment was already on the truck.

Needless to say, it was not uncommon for an unscrupulous estimator to "low-ball" an estimate. A person would often select the company which gave the lowest cost figure. A "Bad News Phone Call" would often follow after the truck was placed on a scale. The household that was supposed to weigh 4000 pounds and cost $2000 to move, mysteriously became 6000 pounds on moving day. The actual cost became considerably higher. It was the driver's duty to inform you of the actual cost, usually by telephone. Many times there were gross differences between what the representative estimated and the total cost you were expected to pay. You would receive a "Bad News Phone Call" - such as "Mrs. Jones, this is the driver. I've got some bad news for you!" This type of scenario occurred too frequently. Many people were without sufficient funds when the truck arrived at destination.

With this type of situation, the driver would not unload the shipment until he was presented with cash or a certified check for the total amount. If the individual could not obtain the exact amount, the driver would not unload. Crying did not help

18

"What do you mean, it's *only* $1000 more?"

the situation! The driver would go to a storage facility and place the shipment under "lock and key". In order to get possession, the person eventually had to pay the entire amount. In addition, the person owed the cost for storage and the cost to move everything into the new home. It was a real "horror story". A long-distance call to the estimator who made the "mistake" would not release you of your financial obligation.

In order to alleviate the hopeless dilemma a number of people got caught up in, the I.C.C. established a rule which protected the consumer from gross miscalculations by the moving company. On all written estimates, it required the total due when the driver arrived, to be no more than the total estimated amount, plus 10%. If the estimator figured the total cost of the move to be $2,000, the driver had to unload if the shipper gave him $2200 (10% more than the total estimated amount).

This was a rule, even if the shipment weighed significantly more, and the actual amount owed was $3,000. On all estimate forms used for interstate moves, a little box was provided for the estimator to write the total figure with the 10% added in. The driver was obligated to relinquish the shipment if that amount was paid upon arrival. The shipper was still obligated to pay the full amount, but had a few weeks to send a check to the company for the additional amount.

Today, the practice of weighing a shipment and paying the total amount based on actual weight, is still a standard method. The estimated amount, plus 10% is still an I.C.C. rule. A person now has 30 days to send a check for the amount which exceeds the estimate, plus 10%.

What you are about to learn are the alternate routes to take! Why should you pay more than initially estimated, simply because mistakes and miscalculations are made by the moving company?

SECTION 2

THE NEW GAME IN TOWN !

" Now, we can have our cake, and eat it, too."
   - Carl and Alma, a retired couple, whose last move was 22 years ago.

Now, for the good part! Enough time has been devoted to explaining standard procedures for pricing interstate moves. *You can save money by not following the standard methods. Thanks to deregulation, there are alternatives.* Anyone who pays attention and learns the rules of the new game in town, can usually save a tremendous amount of money. In addition, all of the uncertainties previously outlined can be eliminated.

Today, it is possible to know the exact cost of a move, without having the household goods placed on a scale. Forget the unfortunate experience that may have happened to you or an acquaintance prior to deregulation. You can now have the moving company and the representative who does the estimating, pay for their own mistakes or miscalculations. Negative newspaper or magazine articles concerning the moving industry, prior to 1980, can be thrown into the nearest trash can or retained for their antique value. Everything has dramatically changed to benefit the consumer.

21

Each company has its own set of rules, regulations and services contained in its I.C.C. tariff book. Most companies have similar rules, but since they each apply on an individual basis, not all are exactly the same. Some offer "services" that others do not provide. The Binding estimate is an example. (Most companies exclude shipments to or from Alaska and Hawaii when providing this "service" as well as others.)

This type of estimate is simply a written estimate, signed by the representative of a company, stating the exact amount you are expected to pay. A company is not obligated to provide this "service", but most major companies do. They may be entitled to charge a small fee, but most do not! *You will find a list of companies which provide this type of estimate, in the following section.*

The significance of a Binding estimate should be obvious. There is no longer a need for a distressed family to pay more than a company originally estimated. Gone are the days when furniture was "held hostage".

The Winds of Deregulation have blown through the moving industry, as well as many others. Today, the I.C.C. rate books are still utilized, but are not always the final word on pricing. Many companies are allowed to negotiate —not a well-publicized fact, but still true.

The Binding estimate eliminates all uncertainties related to cost. With that out of the way, one can attend to the other apprehensions and anxieties related to relocating. If you have ever moved, even across the street, you are aware of what those little details can blossom into. The last thing needed to preoccupy your mind is the worry that final costs will be considerably more than your budget can accommodate. Last, but not least, *with this type of estimate a company may offer "discounts" to a customer.* More on this subject will follow in the next sections.

You now have the essential facts of life for the interstate moving industry. First, a company may offer a guaranteed price in the form of a Binding estimate. Secondly, the pricing does not always have to "go by the book". Armed with these facts, you are ready to start the ball rolling.

"My mother said there would be days like this!"

SECTION 3

SELECTING THE "RIGHT COMPANY"

"Let me introduce you to Mr. Smart."
- The Author

There is no ideal or "best" way for anyone to relocate. Situations will vary from one family to another. However, one aspect is basic to all relocations. Everybody must pay large sums of money to accomplish this nerve-racking experience. Even if you decide to do it yourself, it will be very expensive and extremely aggravating. It is always a "no-win situation".

Let's look at what an informed customer might do upon learning an interstate move is on the horizon. First of all, finding the "best" company is always a difficult task, even for seasoned veterans. Realizing this, a smart shopper begins investigating with a simple word-of-mouth survey. Interviews are conducted with friends, family members and neighbors who moved recently. Who has had remarkably good or bad experiences is quickly discovered. If a particular company is consistently recommended, that firm is placed at the top of the list. Using this method, our educated customer hears a few "horror stories" and some tales of praise. Obvious rejects are weeded out. Next, the Yellow Pages from the local area are utilized to find the names and telephone numbers of companies capable of accomplishing an interstate move.

At this point, calls to both the local Chamber of Commerce and the Better Business Bureau are useful in narrowing the list. While membership in either of these organizations does not mean a company is perfect, it does indicate which companies are "reputation-conscious". The Better Business Bureau can be helpful in defining the nature of complaints a company has received from past customers.

It is important to remember that "people move furniture, and people are only human". This commentary is not included to frighten anyone. It is important to realize that mistakes can be made by the most experienced of professionals in any business. Using professionals will certainly minimize the possibility of damage to your furniture and your body.

By this time, the search focuses on 3 or 4 companies with the best reputation or at least the fewest complaints. A great deal can be learned from a simple phone call to each office. The wise customer notices how the call is handled from the moment the phone is answered. While courteous replies are no guarantee of good service in the future, rude telephone manners often indicate similar behavior later on "down the road".

Mr. Smart then asks a simple question to help determine whether he will consider doing business with the company – "Does your company provide guaranteed prices and/or other types of discounts on interstate relocations?" If the answer is negative, he simply thanks the person and continues the search. *Mr. Smart knows that the Binding estimate can be one of the essential tools needed to get more for his moving dollar.* Assuming the answer is "yes", and most likely it will be, the next question is also important – "Does your company transport *directly* to the area where the household goods will be delivered?" This may seem insignificant, but it is equally critical in the search. Not all companies are permitted to transport into every state. The best company in the world cannot help you, if it is not allowed to deliver into the destination state. The company usually handles this situation by "relaying" the shipment to a state where it is allowed to operate. Mr. Smart knows he wants his things handled as few times as possible. The less handling, the less chance of damage! Therefore, always give top priority to a company authorized to operate *directly* to destination.

The search starts well in advance of the anticipated move (2 months, if possible). Even if Mr. Smart previously used the services of a particular company, he knows the importance of using the elimination process. He wants an objective analysis of which company will provide the best services, has the best safety record, and gives the most reasonable price. This takes time!

The search should lead to at least 3 reputable companies when the process is complete. It will be those companies which come to the residence to discuss their services and give the Binding estimate. (There are a few other types of "discounted estimates" being offered by some companies. Rather than confuse you, the alternatives are explained in a later section. If you have a firm grip on the process involved, the alternatives will be easier to grasp!)

If the answers received on the telephone are satisfactory, Mr. Smart requests that a representative from the company visit his home (at least three different companies). The representative

---

Remember S.O.A.P.

S = Shop
O = Organize
A = Ask questions
P = Plan

---

may be called a sales rep., an estimator or a moving consultant. That person will have three tasks to accomplish. Initially, to discover the needs of Mr. Smart. Secondly, explain how the company can service those needs; and finally, to itemize the cost for those services.

The wise customer tries to schedule all appointments on the same day, or at least within a few days of each other. Enough time is allowed between appointments for each person to do a thorough job (2 hour intervals). The reason is both for convenience, and also to help gain bargaining leverage. If the representatives know that one company has just left and another is on the way, it will become apparent they are dealing with a "serious shopper". This can sometimes produce a lower cost estimate, or at least their "best shot".

This little golden nugget of knowledge is applicable in almost any situation when dealing directly with salespeople. It is valid when purchasing most services. Salespeople usually have some degree of flexibility. Their pricing will often be dictated by the competition. Believe me, this type of strategy does work to get the "best price a salesperson has to offer".

When buying any service, most salesmen will admit that most consumers never receive the salesperson's best price. Consumers are simply not taught to negotiate, as well as salesmen are taught to sell !

The following is a partial list of companies presently allowed to give Binding estimates and/or other discounted types of estimates on interstate moves:

Mayflower	Red Ball
Allied	Global
United	National
North American	Wheaton
Bekins	Lyons
Atlas	Arpin
Burnham	Graebel

28

Most of the interstate companies are organized in a network of agents. For instance, John Smith Moving and Storage may also be known as Smith-Mayflower. Big Apple Moving and Storage may be called Big Apple-United. They act as agents for the national company. Each agent within the various networks has a different performance record. Some are superior, while others barely attain mediocrity. For this reason, even though estimates are received from some of the most recognized names in the industry, it is still worth talking to people in the community to ascertain the reputation of a particular agency. It will be employees or contractors affiliated with the local agent who may be providing services at origin. This is especially true if packing of boxes is requested.

After using the process of elimination, one can never be 100% sure if the right decision is made. The idea is to educate yourself! Try your hardest to make a wise decision.

Most major companies send fancy brochures to a residence once a "For Sale" sign is erected. All claim to be "the best in the industry", or some facsimile close to that. They each have their own fancy names for various services. The "no other company does it better" statement usually prevails. Each representative who enters a home to provide an estimate will proclaim the same loyal company attitude. Certainly, a salesperson will not come to a residence to sell the "second-rate" service offered by the company. Therefore, try to be as objective as possible in making a final selection. Some companies do provide better services than others. They are not all alike! Listen to all of the facts and benefits, not the sales-hype. *I recommend not basing the final decision on who will be the cheapest. Bad service is never worth one thin dime.* (More on this subject is in sub-section entitled, "The Too Good To Be True Binding Estimate".)

THE PERFORMANCE REPORT

Each moving company that transported more than 100 interstate household goods shipments during the prior year, is required to prepare its own performance report. You should receive this when getting the written estimate. It is data supplied by the company which details its performance during the previous year. This allows you to compare each company under consideration.

When trying to formulate an opinion, the report can be a useful tool. However, the statistics are compiled by the company, then submitted to the I.C.C. Unless there are gross overstatements or understatements, don't expect the I.C.C. staff to "burn the midnight oil" trying to discover inaccuracies.

Each company tries to display better percentages than the competition. Under these circumstances, impartiality is hard to avoid. Therefore, use these statistics as a guideline while continuing to gather information from other sources.

The report contains pertinent information such as: how often it was late with either pickups or deliveries; percentage of shipments which did not result in property loss or damage in excess of $100; the average number of days it took to settle claims in excess of $100.

SECTION 4

WHAT TO EXPECT FROM THE PROFESSIONALS

"I know you are willing to give me a 20% discount, but the other company said it is offering a special 30% off sale this month."
— *Mr. Smart, when he was negotiating the price with the second company to provide a cost estimate.*

Now that you have selected three or four companies to send a salesperson to your home, it is helpful to understand who the representative is, and what he or she does. (By the way, there are many qualified women in the industry today.) They are people who regard their jobs as professionals, and act accordingly. Try to mentally rate the degree of professionalism displayed by each individual. That person is the one you will be dealing with until your belongings leave town. Be inquisitive, and ask how long they have been working with their company.

The initial chore will be to take a room-by-room survey of all items to be moved. Before the representative arrives, discuss the move with all family members. Find out exactly what each person intends to take, and what will be discarded. This will be very helpful to you and the estimator.

Each will bring certain items which are "tools-of-the-trade"; a clipboard with a detailed survey sheet attached, the price estimate sheet, and a large book (Tariff Book). This book contains the published rates for moving any amount of weight/cubic feet, any distance between two or more states. The task will be to calculate the weight and amount of space (cubic feet) of each item to be moved. A total for all items, times the "rate"(in dollars and cents, for each 100 pounds), will be arrived at by the estimator.

Review the inventory with the representative. It will be this inventory the driver will evaluate on the morning your shipment is loaded on the truck. He will take his own inventory at that time and compare the results. If any major discrepancies appear, you may have headaches that only the original Watergate conspirators could describe. He may refuse to load items not listed, especially if any price guarantees were given. In addition, he may call his dispatcher requesting the representative be sent to your home to decipher the inconsistencies. Therefore, be honest and you will not have problems. If there are only a few small items, the movers probably will not get annoyed. To avoid hassles on moving day, make sure the survey is complete and accurate. Simply, it is not worth the trauma!

The representative may ask you to place your signature at the bottom of the survey sheet. Your signature indicates you understand that only the articles listed on the form are to be moved at the estimated price. Never sign the form until you are certain all items are listed. Small things that will conveniently fit in a box need not be individually listed. For those items, the estimator will make an educated guess at the total number of boxes needed. This is a game of averages. There is no way of knowing the size of boxes you might use when packing yourself.

Insist on receiving a legible copy of this survey. Since most forms are carbon copies, ask for one which can be read without the use of a magnifying glass. This is the only proof you have to determine what will be moved at the price the representative established. It is also used to determine the amount of space needed on the truck.

THE BINDING (GUARANTEED) ESTIMATE

After the survey has been completed, the estimator will prepare a cost estimate for all services requested or needed. It is now time to develop your negotiating skills! Now, you can "have your cake and eat it, too". It is the best of all possible worlds for the consumer. You can obtain a discount, and at the same time have the price "locked-in".

This concept is somewhat new to the industry. If there is only one or two companies in your area allowed to transport into a particular state, there is a remote possibility you may be charged full price for the move. Also, there is a good chance those companies may not want to give a Binding price. Although this may be allowed by the I.C.C., they may not need to do so. They usually follow what the competition is providing. In a small town, competition is not as fierce as in a large metropolitan area. They are aware they have the "market cornered", and are enjoying the financial rewards. If this is happening in your community, PLEASE READ THE GUARANTEE IN THE FRONT OF THIS BOOK, so as not to be disappointed after putting in the effort.

You may have to be the pioneer in your community who initiates the discussion of providing discounts. Remember, the I.C.C. does allow most of the larger interstate companies to negotiate.

The dollar amount a company will discount depends strictly on how competitive the agents are in your area. It also hinges on how good you are at "negotiating".

Do not be afraid to ask the representatives exactly what percentage has been discounted from the published rates. Most estimators have pressure placed on them to "book the business" at the highest level of profitability. However, they often have flexibility to reduce transportation rates if they feel it is necessary to secure business. It is up to you to let them know of your intentions to get at least three other estimates. You are comparing the cost, as well as the quality of services each company has to offer. Both are of major importance since you will be entrusting all of your worldly possessions with the one selected.

If you presently live in a large metropolitan area with an abundance of companies to choose from, many are already guaranteeing prices for transportation which are less than their I.C.C. tariff book states. Ask to see the rate listed in their books. If you notice they are still using the tariff rate when providing a Binding estimate, inform them of Deregulation. Also, inform the representative you intend to continue entertaining bids from other firms.

Do not get mad at the representatives! Many times, they simply follow instructions given by a sales manager or owner of the company. They dictate the amount of latitude a salesperson has when negotiating prices. They establish the degree of profitability the company can live with. Some firms provide a representative with more flexibility than others.

In a highly competitive community, many estimators provide discounted prices without the customer having to ask. They are aware of what their competitors are doing. They know what the average discount is in the area. Potential customers merely have to state they are "shopping" for the best price and the best services. Estimators realize if they do not come close in price with other major companies, they are not going to get the business.

Since most estimators get paid on a commission basis, you can believe they want your business. They quickly become equally interested in providing the most reasonable price. It is your job to let them know you want them to "give it their best shot". When the estimating job has been completed, the total cost is of monumental importance, as well as quality service. If you have done your homework, as suggested earlier, only companies with a reputation for providing quality service would have been invited to your residence to begin with.

NEGOTIATING OTHER SERVICES

You may request a company to provide additional services other than transportation. First, find out what services are available and the individual costs for such services. Make certain each service is individually listed on the estimate form, and the separate cost for the service is itemized. Do not accept as estimate with nothing but a series of little squares checked-off opposite an extra service. You have a right to know the individual charge for the service requested.

Some hasty estimators may place a total dollar amount on the last line of the form. This makes it very difficult to determine individual costs. You want this information so you can scrutinize these figures with other estimates. Also, if you decide to delete a particular service from the total, you should know exactly how many dollars the estimator will be deducting. *You want everything itemized and each little detail in writing.* Never settle for less. Compare apples with apples!

BOXES AND PACKING LABOR COSTS

Before the representative arrives, decide what you intend to pack, and what you want professionally packed. In order to accurately estimate packing costs, the representative will open closets, cupboards, and china cabinets to survey those items. After the survey, packing costs will be itemized and added to the total. The cost will include:

1. The price for each box (based on size)
2. The cost to pack each box (based on size)

The prices for all boxes are contained in each tariff book, and are the same throughout the country. Packing and unpacking labor charges are also in each tariff book, but these prices can vary slightly from one county to another. If you requested a Binding estimate, you may be able to negotiate a discount on boxes, as well as packing labor costs.

The percentage the representative is willing to reduce these costs depends strictly on the competitive nature of the situation. In principle, it is the same as negotiating the transportation cost.

THE BINDING FORM

After patiently listening to all of the representatives, you will undoubtedly formulate opinions about each company. Also you will probably discover a significant variance in the totals. CONGRATULATIONS! You are half-way home. In order to successfully complete the other half of the journey, devote enough time to analyzing the estimate form.

Discuss all details with the estimator before signing. When you place your signature on this form, you are stating that you are aware the *Binding price is for only those services listed.* Any additional services needed in the future will cost more. You can always add or delete services after signing. This can be accomplished by using a form called an "Addendum". (This is discussed in the following sub-section.) If changes are necessary, notify the representative to prepare this form well in advance of moving day.

THE "ADDENDUM"

(Making Changes After Inventory/Estimate/ Order-for-Service Are Signed)

When the original inventory was taken, there may have been uncertainty concerning what items would be needed in your new home. Maybe you were trying to sell appliances, sofas, etc. Possibly a garage sale was on the horizon. This is a frequent dilemma. Therefore, as you get close to the actual moving date, call the representative who took the survey and inform him or her of changes in the inventory. Additions may increase the price originally received. At the same time, deletions can sometimes result in a decrease in the total cost.

36

For this reason, without writing a totally new estimate, the representative can make the necessary minor adjustments on a form known as the "addendum".

If the weight increases, you can usually expect the cost to go up. However, if items were eliminated, ask the representative to reduce the total to reflect the weight reduction (A big exception to this is explained in sub-section entitled the "Break - Point".) Each of you signs the addendum which states the new agreed upon price for the move. *Never sign an addendum that is blank!*

Depending on circumstances, you may want or need to have additional services performed that initially you were either unsure or unaware of. This is very common when you do not already have a residence at destination. A"stair carry", "long distance carry", or small truck to "shuttle" your belongings an excessive distance may be needed. The addendum can also be utilized for these minor changes, without completely rewriting all of the paperwork.

Do not wait until the last minute to make changes, since it usually requires a return visit by the estimator. In addition, the dispatcher (person who assigns the trucks) may need to send a different truck if there are major changes in the size of the load.

THE "ORDER-FOR-SERVICE" FORM

In most instances, you should not place your signature on an "order-for-service" until receiving a minimum of three estimates. (One major exception to this is explained in sub-section "How Long Is The Price Guaranteed For?" You need ample time to analyze each one, line by line. You may not want to move with the cheapest, especially if you received a negative feeling from the representative.

The salesperson's (estimator/representative) first priority will be to fully convince you that his or her company will provide the best service. If you do not believe that, forget about giving the company your business regardless of price. You can never be assured of a trouble-free move, but you can take precautions to minimize the likelihood of unnecessary problems.

The order form states all of the known details for your relocation: addresses, phone numbers, arranged dates for pickup and delivery, special services, liability coverage, method of payment, etc. Unless you plan to move within a very short period of time (one or two weeks) or have a very small shipment, wait until you know the exact dates you would like scheduled, before signing. Most of the larger companies can usually schedule the loading of an average-sized household with two weeks' notification, going anywhere in the country. Do not get pressured into signing an order-for-service when the estimate is provided. It is unnecessary unless a truck is needed at your door within a few days. It does not benefit you, but in fact, shows you are not following the tactics outlined to negotiate the most reasonable price. You have not done enough "shopping"! This is necessary to get the best service for the least price.

Allow at least three companies an opportunity to explain their services and prices. Whichever representative you ultimately select will be overjoyed to return on another day to complete the order form. Let each one know you are a "tough cookie". In the future, you may even be rewarded by receiving a lower cost estimate from the same company. Believe me, it is happening out there!! The "friendly competition" between companies is unbelievable. Your pocketbook/wallet can benefit if you play the game correctly. Deregulation has given consumers an opportunity to use some strategy. If you follow the game plan, you will get a touch-down and have enough money left over to purchase many hot dogs after the game!

Once you have selected the "right company", have the estimator return. Provide all information which is known at that time. If you must cancel the move for any reason, call the representative immediately. Cancellations and delays are a common occurrence in the moving industry. Therefore, do not be afraid to sign an order-for-service *once you have done your homework.*

THE "BILL OF LADING" (CONTRACT)

The document signed on moving day which legally obligates you and the moving company, is called the "Bill of Lading". *This form is the contract between you and the company.* All details should correspond with information shown on the order-for-service and the estimate. If an addendum was needed, details listed on that form should also be on the Bill of Lading.

Before the driver begins loading, he is required to get this form signed. He will give you a copy. If you do not agree with everything stated, do not sign it. It states what services and liability coverage the company is providing, and prices for those services. It also states the company's responsibilities, as well as your responsibilities to the company. Keep this in a safe place, and have it handy when the shipment is delivered. You may also need this form after delivery if claims need to be settled. Let's hope that is not the case.

THE DRIVER'S INVENTORY

When the driver arrives on moving day, his first chore will be to inventory all items to be moved. The I.C.C. does not require this; however, most drivers will perform their own inventory in case future damage claims are filed. The driver also wants to make sure that what he will be hauling corresponds with the inventory taken by the representative.

He will systematically tour your home, placing self-sticking tags on all boxes and items to be loaded. Each numbered line on the inventory sheet should have a description of the item as well as the present condition. Usually, abbreviations are used to denote present condition. He will be looking for scratches, dents, nicks, etc. *You should accompany the person performing the inventory.* Be certain you agree with the abbreviations used to denote present condition. If you disagree with any description, make your own notation on all copies. Write how you would describe the condition on the same line, and then, place your initials beside the notation.

TABLE OF MEASUREMENTS

NAME OF CARRIER **ABC Moving Co.** DATE **1, 17,** 19 **88**

SHIPPER **Phil and Elaine Rummuno** PHONE **715-9580** CONSIGNEE **same**

SHIPMENT MOVING FROM **Los Angeles, CA.** TO **Buffalo, N.Y.**

LIVING ROOM

Article	No.	Cu	Tot
Bar, Portable		15	
Bench, Frnd/Piano		5	
Bookcase	2	20	40
Bookshelves, Sect.		5	
Cabinet, Curio		10	
Chair, Straight		5	
Chair, Arm		10	
Chair, Rocker		12	
Chair, Occasional	1	15	15
Chair, Overstuffed		25	
Chest, Cedar		15	
Clock, Grandfather		20	
Day Bed		30	
Desk, SM/Winthrop		22	
Desk, Secretary		35	
Fireplace Equip.		5	
Footstool	1	2	2
Hall Tree Rack		2	
Hall Tree Large		12	
Lamp, Floor		3	
Lamp, Pole		3	
Magazine Rack		2	
Music Cabinet		10	
Piano, Baby Gr/Upr		70	
Piano, Parlor Gr.		80	
Piano, Spinet/Console		60	
Radio, Table		2	
Rec. Player, Port.		2	
Rugs, Lg. Roll/Pad		10	
Rugs, Sm. Roll/Pad		3	
Sofa, Rattan/Wicker		10	
Sofa, Sec., Per Sec.		30	
Sofa, Loveseat	2	35	70
Sofa, 3 Cushion		50	
Sofa, Hide, 4 Cush.		60	
Stereo Component		8	
Stereo Console		15	
Tables, Drop/Occas		12	
Tables, Coffee		5	
Tables, End		5	
Telephone Stand		5	
TV, Portable		5	
TV, Table Model	2	10	20
TV, Console		15	
TV, Combination		25	
TV, Stand		3	
Trunk		5	

DINING ROOM

Article	No.	Cu	Tot
Bench, Harvest		10	
Buffet (Base)		30	
Hutch (Top)		20	
Cabinet, Corner		20	
Dining Table	1	30	30
Dining Chair	6	5	30
Server		15	
Tea Cart		10	
Rugs, Pad Large		10	
Rugs, Pad Small		3	
Total Col. 1	**15**		**207**

Carton	Carr. Pack	Own. Pack	Tot. Ctn.	Cb	Tot. Cb
Dish-pack				10	
	3	3	10	30	
Carton 1.5			10		
	5	5	1.5	8	
			1.5		
			1.5		
Carton 3.0	10	10	3.0	30	
			3.0		
			3.0		
Carton 4.5	10	10	4.5	45	
			4.5		
			4.5		
Carton 6.0			6.0		
			6.0		
			6.0		
Wardrobe	2		2	10	20
Crib Matt.					
Single Matt.					
Dbl. Matt.					
Qn/Kg. Matt.					
Mirror Ctn.	3		3	(2)	6
Crates					
Total	**33**			**139**	

BEDROOM

Article	No.	Cu	Tot
Bed Incl Sp/Matt			
Bed, Waterbed Base		10	
Bed, Rollaway		20	
Bed, Single/Hollywood		40	
Bed, Std/Dbl.		60	
Bed, Queen		65	
Bed, King		70	
Bed, Bunk (Set 2)		70	
Bookshelves, Sect.		5	
Chair, Boudoir		10	
Chair, Str/Rocker		5	
Chaise Lounge		25	
Chest, Bachelor		12	
Chest, Cedar		15	
Chest, Armoire		30	
Desk, SM/Winthrop		22	
Dresser/Vanity Bch		3	
Dresser, Vanity		20	
Dresser, Single		30	
Dresser, Double		40	
Dresser, Triple		50	
Night Table		5	
Rug, Large or Pad		10	
Rug, Small or Pad		3	
Wardrobe, Small		20	
Wardrobe, Large		40	

NURSERY

Article	No.	Cu	Tot
Bathinette		5	
Bed, Youth		30	
Chair, Childs		3	
Chair, High		5	
Chest		12	
Chest, Toy		5	
Crib, Baby		10	
Table, Childs		5	
Playpen		10	
Rug, Large or Pad		10	
Rug, Small or Pad	2	3	6

APPLIANCES

Article	No.	Cu	Tot
Air Cond/Window Sm		15	
Air Cond/Window La.		20	
Dehumidifier		10	
Dishwasher		20	
Freezer			
Freezer, 10 or less		30	
Freezer, 11 to 15		45	
Freezer, 16 or Over		60	
Range, 20" Wide		10	
Range, 30" Wide		15	
Range, 36" Wide		30	
Refrigerator (CuCp)			
Refrigerator, 6cu.ft.or less		30	
Refrigerator, 7 to 10cu.ft.		45	
Refrigerator, 11 cu.ft./over		60	
Trash Compactor		15	
Vacuum Cleaner	2	5	10
Washing Machine		25	
Dryer	1	25	25

KITCHEN

Article	No.	Cu	Tot
Bkft. Suite, Chairs	4	5	20
Breakfast Table		10	10
Chair, High		5	
Ironing Board	1	2	2
Kitchen Cabinet		30	
Microwave Oven		10	
Serving Cart		15	
Stool		3	
Table		5	
Utility Cabinet		10	
Total Col. 2	**11**		**73**

Enter item and cube under "Miscellaneous" in addition to completing below:

Boat Linear Ft. ___ x 115 = ___ lbs.			
Boat Trlr. Lin. Ft. ___ x 75 = ___ lbs.			
Sailboat Lin. Ft. ___ x 125 = ___ lbs.			
Other ___ Lin. Ft. ___ x ___ = ___ lbs.			
Total Wt. Additive			

Signing below acknowledges receipt of an estimate of your move based on the Table of Measurements and other information. Only the items listed are included in the cost. Any items or additional services added may result in additional cost.

✱

Shipper ___ **1/17/88** Date

Carrier's Representative **Henry Costantino**

PORCH & OUTDOOR

Article	No.	Cu	Tot
BBQ Grill, Small		2	
BBQ Grill, Large	1	10	10
Chairs, Aluminum		1	
Chairs, Metal		3	
Chairs, Wood	2	5	10
Gard. Hose & Tools		10	
Glider or Settee		20	
Ladder, 6' Step		3	
Ladder, 8' Metal		2	
Ladder, Extension		8	
Lawn Mower, Hand		6	
Lawn Mower, Power		15	
Lawn Mower, Riding (HP)		35	
Leaf Sweeper		5	
Outdoor Child Slide		10	
Outdoor Child Gym		20	
Outdoor Drv. Racks		25	
Outdoor Swings		30	
Picnic Table		20	
Picnic Bench		5	
Roller, Lawn		15	
Rug, Large		7	
Rug, Small		3	
Sand Box		10	
Spreader		2	
Table, Small		2	
Table, Large		4	
Umbrella	1	5	5
Wheelbarrow	1	8	8

MISCELLANEOUS

Article	No.	Cu	Tot
Baby Carriage		4	
Barbells ___ lbs.			
Basket (Clothes)		5	
Bicycle		5	
Tricycle		2	
Bowling Ball/Bag		3	
Card Table		2	
Folding Chairs	4	1	4
Clothes Hamper		5	
Cot, Folding		5	
Desk, Office		30	
Fan		5	
Fern/Plant Stands		2	
Filing Cab. Crdbd.		3	
Filing Cab. 2 door		10	
Filing Cab. 4 door		20	
Footlockers		5	
Game Table		15	
Golf Bag	2	4	8
Heater, Gas/Elec.		5	
Metal Shelves		5	
Ping Pong Table		40	
Pool Table Comp.		40	
Pool Table Slate		100	
Power Tool Hand Ea		3	
Power Tool Stand		15	
Sewing Mach., Port		5	
Sewing Mach., Console		10	
Sewing Mach. w/Cabinet		20	
Sled		2	
Suitcase		5	
Table, Utility		5	
Tackle Box		1	
Tire		3	
Tire w/Rim		5	
Toolchest, Small		5	
Toolchest, Medium		10	
Toolchest, Large		15	
Trash Can		7	
Wagon, Child's		5	
Wastepaper Basket	1	2	2
Work Bench		20	

	PCS	CUBE
Total This Column	12	47
Total Col. 1	15	207
Total Col. 2	11	73
Total Cartons	33	139
Total	71	466

Wt. Factor (lbs/cu. ft.) **466 cubic ft.**

Computed Est. Wt. **3200 pounds**

Total Wt. Additive ___

Total Est. Weight **3200 pounds**

Table of Measurements (Survey) – When the estimator tours your home, every item to be placed on the truck will be listed. This survey will be used to determine the amount of space neeeded on the truck (cubic feet), as well as the total weight.

ESTIMATED CHARGES FOR **LEONARD WRATE** PACKING DATE **1/17/88**

ESTIMATED COST OF SERVICE (Based on tariff **400-C** TRANS. RATE SECTION **3**)

Tariff Item No.

TRANSPORTATION:

No. Items _____ cu. ft. _____ @ _____ ¢ per cu. ft. = _____ $ _____

130 Bulky Article (Describe) _____ Wt. Additive (when applicable) _____ Ld/unld-HDLG. CHG. (When Applicable) _____

Total Estimate Wt. _____

☐ Exclusive Use _____ Cu. Ft. Van   ☐ Expedited Service _____ Lbs./Minimum

☐ Space Reservation _____ Cu. Ft.   ☐ Day Certain Loading _____ Min. Wgt.

Estimated Trans. Chg. **4000#** , **2056** miles @ $ **$20.** Per Cwt. **800.00**

Seasonal Rate Adjustment % _____

170 Additional Transportation (Origin) **SAN DIEGO COUNTY #1.00 cwt** **40.00**

170 Additional Transportation (Destination) **ERIE COUNTY #1.25 cwt** **50.00**

STORAGE: (Lbs _____) ORIGIN ☐ DESTINATION ☐

Sec. 9 Transportation In or Out of Warehouse _____ Miles _____ Rt./Cwt. _____

185 Days in Storage _____ 1st Day Rate _____ Additional Day Rate _____

185 Warehouse Handling Rt./Cwt. _____

190 **VALUATION:**

Transportation Portion $/Lb. _____ Valuation **10,000.** Rt./$100 $ **50** **50.00**

SIT Portion (ECL) _____

ADDITIONAL SERVICES:

115 Extra Pickup Nbr. _____ Address _____

115 Extra Delivery Nbr. _____ Address _____

195 Appliance Service (Origin) Nbr. _____ (If third party, enter under misc. charges) _____

195 Appliance Service (Destination) Nbr. _____ (If third party, enter under misc. charges) _____

135 Piano Less than 38" ☐ Over 38" ☐ Handling Charge _____

Flight Carry: No. Flights _____ @ $ _____ 1st. Flight; $ _____ Each Addtl. Flight _____

Packing Containers (see detail below) _____

Packing Service (see detail below) _____

Unpacking Service (see detail below) _____

120 Extra Labor (Origin) Nbr. Men _____ Hrs. _____ TOTAL MAN HOURS _____ @ $ _____ PER MAN HOUR

120 Extra Labor (Destination) Nbr. Men _____ Hrs. _____ TOTAL MAN HOURS _____ @ $ _____ PER MAN HOUR

160 Long Carry Weight _____ Total Distance _____ ft. No. Carriers _____ Rate per Cwt per carry _____

160 Flights Weight _____ No. Flts _____ Rate per Cwt per flt. _____

160 Elevator Weight _____ Floor # _____ Rate per Cwt _____

Misc. Charges Itemize _____

TOTAL **940.00**

COST ESTIMATE ☒ WAS ☐ WAS NOT GIVEN TO SHIPPER

☒ TOTAL AMOUNT OF <u>BINDING</u> ESTIMATE $ **940.00**

☐ TOTAL <u>NON-BINDING</u> ESTIMATED COST $ _____

ESTIMATED COST OF CONTAINERS AND PACKING AND UNPACKING SERVICES	CONTAINERS			PACKING (Schedule)			UNPACKING (Schedule)		
	Estimated Number	Per Each	TOTAL	Estimated Number	Per Each	TOTAL	Estimated Number	Per Each	TOTAL
Dish-pack, drum, etc.		$	$		$	$		$	$
Cartons: Less than 3 cubic feet									
3 cubic feet									
4½ cubic feet									
6 cubic feet									
6½ cubic feet									
Wardrobe Carton									
Crib Mattress Carton									
Mattress Carton (not exceeding 39" x 75")									
Mattress Carton (not exceeding 54" x 75")									
Mattress Carton (exceeding 54" x 75")									
Mattress Carton (exceeding 39" x 80")									
Mattress Cover (plastic or paper)									
Corrugated Containers: Specially designed for mirrors, paintings, glass tops, etc.									
Crates. Custom made for mirrors, paintings, glass tops, etc									
	Estimated Container	COSTS $		Estimated Packing	COSTS $		Estimated Unpacking	COSTS $	

AGENCY NAME: **ABC Moving Co., San Diego, CA.**
ADDRESS

David Staso
AGENCY REPRESENTATIVE

Estimate of Cost – All individual charges should be itemized on the estimate.

ORDER FOR SERVICE

Agent ABC Moving Co.   City BUFFALO, NY   Date 1/10/88

SHIP GOODS DESCRIBED BELOW FROM   **FOR TRANSPORTATION AND DELIVERY TO**

Shipper HAROLD AND SYLVIA SIEGEL   Consignee Same

c/o Same   c/o Same or HERMAN and CELIA SIEGEL

Street Address 481 Linwood Ave. Fl. 1st Street Address 47 BEACH WAY Fl. 1st

City & State BUFFALO, NY Tel 503-123-4567   City & State LONG BEACH, CA Tel 805-456-8037

SUBJECT TO THE FOLLOWING CONDITIONS	TYPE OF SHIPMENT COD ☒ Nat. Acct. ☒

Agreed Pick-up Date or Period of Time 1/10/88

Agreed Delivery Date or Period of Time 1/15 - 1/21/88

Moving subject to guaranteed pickup/delivery program ☐

Penalty for delay $_____ per day.

Shipper's Contact Point at DESTINATION (NEIGHBOR-HERMAN OR CELIA) Tel. No. 805-456-9817

Shipper requests notification of charges Yes ☐ No ☒ Same as above ☐ or

at ——— BINDING PRICE ——— Tel. No. _____

Delivering Carrier: SMITH MOVING Co.

Destination Agent XYZ MOVERS

Location LONG BEACH, CA Tel. No. 805-123-4567

DRIVER'S PAPERS

☐ General Delivery ☐ Shipper's House ☒ Origin Agent's Office

☐ Other Agent's Office at _____

Date Registered with General Office _____

BINDING ESTIMATE ☒ YES ☐ NO

THIS BINDING ESTIMATE REPRESENTS THE CHARGES FOR ONLY THOSE SERVICES INDICATED ON THE REVERSE. CHARGES FOR ADDITIONAL SERVICES WILL BE ADDED TO THIS TOTAL.

BINDING TOTAL $ 4,150.00

NON-BINDING ESTIMATE ☐ YES ☒ NO

THIS ESTIMATE COVERS ONLY THE ARTICLES AND SERVICES LISTED. IT IS NOT A GUARANTEE THAT THE ACTUAL CHARGES WILL NOT EXCEED THE AMOUNT OF THE ESTIMATE. COMMON CARRIERS ARE REQUIRED BY LAW TO COLLECT TRANSPORTATION AND OTHER INCIDENTAL CHARGES COMPUTED ON THE BASIS OF RATES SHOWN IN THEIR LAWFULLY PUBLISHED TARIFFS, REGARDLESS OF PRIOR RATE QUOTATIONS OR ESTIMATES MADE BY THE CARRIER OR ITS AGENTS. EXACT CHARGES FOR LOADING, TRANSPORTING, AND UNLOADING ARE BASED UPON THE WEIGHT OF THE GOODS TRANSPORTED, AND SUCH CHARGES MAY NOT BE DETERMINED PRIOR TO THE TIME THE GOODS ARE LOADED ON THE VAN AND WEIGHED. CHARGES FOR ADDITIONAL SERVICES WILL BE ADDED TO THE TRANSPORTATION CHARGES.

ESTIMATED TOTAL _____

IF THE TOTAL TARIFF CHARGES FOR THE LISTED ARTICLES AND SERVICES EXCEED THIS ESTIMATE BY MORE THAN TEN PERCENT, THEN, UPON YOUR REQUEST, THE CARRIER MUST RELINQUISH POSSESSION OF YOUR SHIPMENT UPON PAYMENT OF NOT MORE THAN 110 PERCENT OF ESTIMATED CHARGES. YOU ARE STILL OBLIGATED TO PAY THE BALANCE OF THE TOTAL CHARGES WITHIN 30 DAYS.

MAXIMUM AMOUNT TO BE PAID ON DELIVERY OF YOUR C.O.D. SHIPMENT IN CASH, CERTIFIED CHECK OR MONEY ORDER IS (TOTAL ESTIMATED COST PLUS 10 PERCENT).

MAXIMUM C.O.D. _____

SEE REVERSE FOR ESTIMATED CHARGES AND DESCRIPTION OF SERVICES

CHARGES AND METHOD OF PAYMENT

Minimum Weight none

Minimum Charges none

Cubic Feet 500

Method of Payment C.O.D.

All charges to be paid in cash, money order (other than personal money order) traveler's check, cashier's check, bank treasurer's check, or certified check, made payable to ABC MOVING Co. before property is relinquished by carrier unless otherwise stated.

ON EMPLOYER PAID MOVES, SHIPPER IS LIABLE FOR ALL CARRIER CHARGES IF EMPLOYER FAILS TO MAKE PAYMENT AS PROMISED

Invoice to _____

Address _____

City & State _____

Customer No. _____

COMMENTS _____

VALUATION PROTECTION REQUESTED

Unless the shipper expressly releases the shipment to a value of 60 cents per pound per article, the carrier's maximum liability for loss and damage shall be either the lump sum value declared by the shipper or an amount equal to $1.25 for each pound of weight in the shipment, whichever is greater. The shipment will move subject to the rules and conditions of the carrier's tariff. Shipper hereby releases the entire shipment to a value not exceeding

$ 10,000.00

(to be completed by the person signing below)

NOTICE: The shipper signing this Order For Service must insert in the space above, in his own handwriting, either his declaration of the actual value of the shipment, or the words "60 cents per pound per article." Otherwise the shipment will be deemed released to a maximum value equal to $1.25 times the weight of the shipment in pounds.

REPLACEMENT VALUE PROTECTION

Minimum value-$3.50 per pound or $15,000 whichever is greater

☐ Option A - no deductible   ☐ Option B - $300.00 deductible

The shipper signing this contract must insert, in the space below, his or her declaration of the released value of the shipment. Otherwise, the shipment will be deemed released to a value equal to $3.50 times the weight in pounds. Shipper hereby releases the entire shipment to a value not exceeding $_____

REFER TO THE NUMBER IN ALL COMMUNICATIONS

ORDER FOR SERVICE NO. B-107-60

The undersigned shipper hereby requests the above named carrier to furnish the transportation facilities and services described in this order, subject to the contract terms and conditions of carrier's household goods bill of lading, which bill of lading will be issued at time carrier takes possession of this shipment, and subject to the tariffs of the carrier in effect on the date transportation services commence.

SERVICE CANNOT BE PERFORMED WITHOUT PROPER SIGNATURE OR WRITTEN AUTHORITY This 10 day of JANUARY 19 88

Henry P. Costantino - Sales Rep. ✱ By _____

(Signature of Shipper or Authorized Shipper's Agent)

Order-For-Service – Contains all of the important facts pertaining to your move.

ORDER FOR SERVICE
AND
ESTIMATED COST OF SERVICE ADDENDUM

ORDER NO. A - 5037 - 7143   DATE 1/20/88

This will certify and attest that the shipper or a representative of the shipper on the above noted Order for Service, or Estimate Cost of Service,
Dated 1 - 10 - 88 requests that ABC MOVING Co. make the following changes in the Order for Service and/or Estimate
Cost of Service:

		FROM	TO
AGREED PICK-UP DATE OR PERIOD OF TIME	1	1/25/88	1/28/88
AGREED DELIVERY DATE OR PERIOD OF TIME	2		
TOTAL ESTIMATE COST OF SERVICE (BINDING)	3	$2501.00	$2645.00
IF ESTIMATE CHANGED, INDICATE CHANGE IN CUBES, IF APPLICABLE	4		
ADDITIONAL PACKING ORDERED AT ORIGIN	5		
ADDITIONAL UNPACKING AT DESTINATION	6		

CHANGE IN DESTINATION, CHANGE TO: 7
          STREET _____
          CITY _____
          STATE _____ PHONE _____

SHIPPER'S CONTACT AT DEST. CHANGE TO: 8
          STREET _____
          CITY _____
          STATE _____ PHONE _____

MAXIMUM AMOUNT REQUIRED TO RELINQUISH
POSSESSION OF A C.O.D. SHIPMENT   9 _____ _____

SHIPPER REQUESTS NOTIFICATION OF CHARGES AT: 10
          STREET _____
          CITY _____
          STATE _____ PHONE _____

ABC MOVING Co.
NAME AND LOCATION OF AGENT

Burnice De Spain
SHIPPER OR SHIPPER'S REPRESENTATIVE

Fred Rutabor - Sales Rep.
SIGNATURE OF AGENT'S REPRESENTATIVE

Addendum – States any changes required since the estimate
and/or order-for-service were signed.

BILL OF LADING NO	07-543-1	COMBINED UNIFORM HOUSEHOLD GOODS BILL OF LADING AND FREIGHT BILL NON - NEGOTIABLE		ORDER FOR SERVICE NO. DO NOT ALTER
DATE 1/17/89				A ∙...
ISSUING AGENT ABC Moving Co.				REFER TO THIS NUMBER IN ALL COMMUNICATIONS

RECEIVED, SUBJECT TO CLASSIFICATIONS, TARIFFS, RULES AND REGULATIONS INCLUDING ALL TERMS PRINTED OR STAMPED HEREON OR ON THE REVERSE SIDE HEREOF IN EFFECT ON THE DATE OF ISSUE OF THIS BILL OF LADING.   CONNECTING CARRIER — NONE —

SHIPPER JIM AND MARY ALLEN	CONSIGNEE SAME OR NEIGBORS
LOAD FROM C/O —	DELIVER TO C/O — (NICK AND NANCY MURIELLA)
ADDRESS 25 Caso Ave.	ADDRESS 456 Naper
CITY Mission Viejo, CNTY ORANGE STATE CA	CITY Chicago, CNTY Cook STATE IL
TEL 503-123-1235	TEL 803-123-8765

IN CASE OF NEED CONTACT	AGREED PICK-UP DATE / PER. OF TIME 1/29/88
NAME JANET DELMONTE (her Sister)	ACTUAL PICK-UP DATE
ADDRESS	AGREED DELIVERY DATE / PER OF TIME 2/8/88 - 2/12/88
CITY SAME AS ABOVE STATE	IF GUARANTEED SERVICE, PENALTY PER TARIFF IS $ PER DAY
TEL	

IF SHIPPER REQUESTS NOTICE OF CHARGES ☐ OR IN EVENT OF DELAY ☒ NOTIFY.	ESTIMATED COST: $3,157.00	BINDING: ☒ YES ☐ NO
NAME LINDA ROSSETI	MAX. AMT. REQUIRED (EST. + 10%)	
ADDRESS	TO BE PAID ON DELIVERY. $	BALANCE DUE IN 30 DAYS
CITY STATE	MIN. CHARGE	METHOD OF PAYMENT COD
TEL WORK # — 803-456-1236	BILL TO	

	ORIGINAL	REWEIGH	ADDRESS — COD —
GROSS			CITY STATE
TARE			CUST. NO.
NET			TARIFF TRANS. RATE SEC. OR ITEM NO.
DRIVER NO.		VEHICLE NO.	

CHARGES FOR MATL. PACKING & UNPACKING	CONTAINERS				PACKING SCHEDULE ( )				UNPACKING SCHEDULE ( )			
	AGT / DR	QTY	RATE	CHARGE	AGT / DR	QTY	RATE	CHARGE	AGT / DR	QTY	RATE	CHARGE
DRUM-DISHPACK, Not Less Than 5 Cu. Ft.												
CARTONS Less than 3 Cu. Ft.												
3 Cu. Ft.												
4½ Cu. Ft.												
6 Cu. Ft.												
6½ Cu. Ft.												
WARDROBE CARTONS Not Less Than 10 Cu. Ft.	none				none				none			
MATTRESS CARTONS Not Ex. 39" x 75"												
MATTRESS CARTONS Not Ex. 54" x 75"												
MATTRESS CARTONS Exceeding 54" x 75"												
CORRUGATED CONT												
CRATES Minimum Size												
CRATES Over Minimum Size												
	689 TOTAL				690 TOTAL				691 TOTAL			

UNLESS THE SHIPPER EXPRESSLY RELEASES THE SHIPMENT TO A VALUE OF 60 CENTS PER POUND PER ARTICLE, THE CARRIER'S MAXIMUM LIABILITY FOR LOSS AND DAMAGE SHALL BE EITHER THE LUMP SUM VALUE DECLARED BY THE SHIPPER OR AN AMOUNT EQUAL TO $1.25 FOR EACH POUND OF WEIGHT IN THE SHIPMENT WHICHEVER IS GREATER. THE SHIPMENT WILL MOVE SUBJECT TO THE RULES AND CONDITIONS OF THE CARRIER'S TARIFF. SHIPPER HEREBY RELEASES THE ENTIRE SHIPMENT TO A VALUE NOT EXCEEDING

$ 20,000. —
(to be completed by person signing below)

NOTICE: THE SHIPPER SIGNING THIS CONTRACT MUST INSERT IN THE SPACE ABOVE, IN HIS OWN HANDWRITING, EITHER HIS DECLARATION OF THE ACTUAL VALUE OF THE SHIPMENT OR THE WORDS "60 CENTS PER POUND PER ARTICLE." OTHERWISE THE SHIPMENT WILL BE DEEMED RELEASED TO A MAXIMUM VALUE EQUAL TO $1.25 TIMES THE WEIGHT OF THE SHIPMENT IN POUNDS.

SHIPPER X Jim Allen
DATE 1/29/88

REPLACEMENT VALUE PROTECTION
Minimum value – $3.50 per pound or $15,000, whichever is greater.
☐ Option A - No Deductible
☐ Option B - $300 Deductible

THE SHIPPER SIGNING THIS CONTRACT MUST INSERT IN THE SPACE BELOW, HIS DECLARATION OF THE RELEASED VALUE OF THE SHIPMENT. OTHERWISE, THE SHIPMENT WILL BE DEEMED RELEASED TO A VALUE EQUAL TO $3.50 TIMES THE WEIGHT IN POUNDS OR $15,000, WHICHEVER IS GREATER. SHIPPER HEREBY RELEASES THE ENTIRE SHIPMENT TO A VALUE NOT EXCEEDING $ _____

SHIPPER X _____
DATE _____

Carrier agrees to transport the goods and effects tendered by the shipper subject to the preceding terms and conditions.

X _____
Carrier or Authorized Agent

Leave over ☐ Yes ☐ No

Agents No.	DESCRIPTION	CODE	QUANTITY	RATE	CHARGE
	TOTAL CONTAINERS PACKING & UNPACKING	→			
	TRANSPORTATION 2100 MILES	001			2529.00
	ADD TRANSP. - ORIG. ORANGE Co.	088			150.00
	ADD TRANSP. - DEST. Cook Co.	089			300.00
	ORIGIN TO WAREHOUSE MILES	044			
	WAREHOUSE TO DESTINATION MILES	045			
	STORAGE-IN-TRANSIT	169			
	WAREHOUSE HANDLING	090			
	EXTRA PICKUP(S)	091			
	EXTRA DELIVERY(IES)	092			
	EXTRA LABOR Men Man Hrs.	135			
	FLIGHT CHARGE No.	171			28.00
	EXCESSIVE DISTANCE CARRY Feet	172			
	VALUATION $20,000.	138			100.00
	PIANO HANDLING	094			50.00
	APPLIANCE SERVICING	096			
	ADVANCE CHARGE - ACCOUNT OF	060			
				TOTAL	3,157.00
				PD. TO APPLY	
				BALANCE	

CHARGES TO BE PAID IN CASH, MONEY ORDER (OTHER THAN PERSONAL MONEY ORDER). TRAVELER'S CHECK, CASHIER'S CHECK, MADE PAYABLE TO ABC Moving Co. Inc. BEFORE PROPERTY IS RELINQUISHED BY CARRIER UNLESS OTHERWISE STATED. ON EMPLOYER PAID MOVES, SHIPPER IS LIABLE FOR ALL CARRIER CHARGES IF EMPLOYER FAILS TO MAKE PAYMENT AS PROMISED.

PREPAYMENT $ 3,157.00 RECEIVED BY Nick Shaeb - DRIVER DATE 1/29/88

BALANCE $ NONE — RECEIVED BY _____ DATE _____

THE ABOVE DESCRIBED SHIPMENT WAS RECEIVED IN APPARENT GOOD CONDITION EXCEPT AS NOTED ON THE INVENTORY.

CONSIGNEE OR AGENT OF CONSIGNEE Mary Allen DATE DELIVERED 2/10/88

RECEIVED FOR STORAGE IN TRANSIT AT _____
AGENCY NAME   WAREHOUSE LOCATION   BY   ON   AGENTS SIGNATURE   DATE

BILL OF LADING

Bill of Lading – This is your contract with the moving company. It is signed on moving day, and again upon delivery. Before signing, be sure all details are correct.

HOUSEHOLD GOODS DESCRIPTIVE INVENTORY

CONTRACTOR OR CARRIER ACE MOVING	AGENT DELMONTE VAN LINES
	CARRIER'S REFERENCE NO. G-05-1767
OWNER'S GRADE OR RATING AND NAME DOUGLAS & ELLEN WALKER	CONTRACT OR GBL NO. 556-039
ORIGIN LOADING ADDRESS TORINA CIRCLE (#1), MISSION VIEJO, CA CITY STATE	GOVT. SERVICE ORDER NO.
DESTINATION BUFFALO, N.Y.	VAN NUMBER 127

DESCRIPTIVE SYMBOLS
CP - Packed By Carrier
PBO - Packed By Owner
CD - Carrier Disassembled

DBO - Disassembled by Owner
PB - Professional Books
PP - Professional Papers

PE - Professional Equipment
B&W - TV Black & White
C - TV Color
MCU - Mechanical Condition Unknown

EXCEPTION SYMBOLS
BE - Bent
BR - Broken
BU - Burned
CH - Chipped
CU - Contents and Condition Unknown

D - Dented
F - Faded
G - Gouged
L - Loose
M - Marred
MI - Mildew

MO - Motheaten
R - Rubbed
RU - Rusted
SC - Scratched
SH - Short

SO - Soiled
T - Torn
W - Badly Worn
Z - Cracked

NOTE: The omission of these symbols indicates good condition except for normal wear.

LOCATION SYMBOLS
1 Arm 7 Rear
2 Bottom 8 Right
3 Corner 9 Side
4 Front 10 Top
5 Left 11 Veneer
6 Leg 12 Edge
13 Center

ITEM NO.	STG. CK. / CR. REF.	ARTICLES	CONDITION AT ORIGIN	ROOM	EXCEPTIONS (IF ANY) AT DESTINATION
101		SOFA	SO-7,8 M-6,7,8		
102		LOVE SEAT	T-4,5		
103		DINING ROOM TABLE			
104		" " CHAIR			
105		" " "			
106		" " "			
107		" " "			
108		" " "			
109		" " "			
110		END TABLE	G-6		
111		PLANT STAND	Z-6		
112		PORTABLE T.V.	SC-10		
113		CONSOLE T.V.			
114		ARM CHAIR	(BLUE) W-10		
115		" "			
116		" "			
117		" "			
118		CARTON	PBO		dented on delivery
119		"	"		
120		"	"		
121		"	"		
122		"	"		
123		"	"		
124		"	"		
125		"	"		
126		BED	(DOUBLE) SC-5,6		
127		DRESSER			
128		"			
129		COAT RACK			
130		BENCH			

IMPORTANT NOTICE ➡

BEFORE SIGNING — CHECK SHIPMENT, COUNT ITEMS AND DESCRIBE LOSS OR DAMAGE IN SPACE ON THE RIGHT ABOVE.

"WE HAVE CHECKED ALL THE ITEMS LISTED AND NUMBERED ON THIS PAGE INCLUSIVE AND ACKNOWLEDGE THAT THIS IS A TRUE AND COMPLETE LIST OF THE GOODS TENDERED AND OF THE STATE OF THE GOODS RECEIVED."

AT ORIGIN	LOADING HAULER NAME & NUMBER (Signature) Carl Francis	DATE 2/5/88	AT DESTINATION	DELIVERING HAULER NAME & NUMBER (Signature) Carl Francis -047	DATE 2/10/88
	OWNER OR AUTHORIZED AGENT (Signature) Doug Walker	DATE 2/5/88		OWNER OR AUTHORIZED AGENT (Signature) Doug Walker	DATE 2/10/88

Driver's Inventory – You will sign these sheets before the truck is loaded, and again upon delivery. If you need to make any notations at either end, write them on *all copies*.

Check to make sure all items receive a tag. The driver will sign all copies of the inventory sheets when the process is completed, and you will be asked to place your signature on each sheet. Do not sign until you are certain all items are listed, and the description of condition is accurate. Review your notes on corresponding lines where you disagree with the description.

You should not feel insulted because some stranger is touring your abode proclaiming a favorite family heirloom from your great-grandmother is nicked, scratched, marred, etc. Most older items usually are. Remember, this person is a profess-ional. He is performing as you would expect a professional providing any service. This part of the job is a time-consuming "pain in the tutu". He is trying to be thorough, and as accurate as humanly possible for his protection and yours. He does not want to be blamed for any damage he did not cause.

Most professional movers take great pride in their performance records and do not like them blemished. Therefore, do not engage in an argument with the driver before he starts loading. Make your notations on the inventory, if necessary. Be patient, and remember he is trying to do a complete professional job, from beginning to end. Don't make life difficult for him.

The driver will give you a copy of all pages. Keep the inventory and the Bill of Lading in a convenient place. These papers will be needed when the truck arrives at the new residence.

HOW LONG IS THE PRICE GUARANTEED?

Each company providing guaranteed prices has its terms and conditions outlined in its I.C.C. tariff book. Since each one may offer a small variation, ask enough questions of all representatives to determine what is most acceptable to your particular situation.

With many companies, a Binding price can be locked-in for a period of 60 days from the date an order-for-service is signed by you. Some companies start the count-down from the

46

day you sign the Binding estimate form. In either case, having this 60-day "grace period" is extremely important to you. If the transportation rate or cost for other itemized services should increase during that 60-day period, most companies only require you to pay the rates in effect on the day you signed.

When you are receiving a Binding estimate, ask the representatives if their company anticipates (or has already received approval from the I.C.C.) for a rate increase in the near future. If so, you may want to accelerate your efforts to select and sign up with a particular company, *providing its "company policy" is to not include increases which may go into effect during the 60-day period after you signed up with its guaranteed price program.*

If the person providing the price guarantee is aware of a pending rate increase, he/she may have to adhere to a "company policy" which can differ from other companies. Some will tell their representatives that they must include all approved rate increases into all estimates, even when those rates are not yet in effect, but will be on the day of the move. On the other hand, some have a policy of honoring prices for 60 days from the day you sign up, irregardless of what may happen to the rates within that time period. Therefore, ask each representative about present "company policy", and be sure to "shop around".

Call the representative of the company you selected, about two weeks before moving day. Get verification that the "company policy" did not mysteriously change. If it did, and you were not given the courtesy of a telephone call to inform you, consider calling the moving company that was your "second choice". You can cancel an order-for-service without financial penalties. All moving companies are aware that many circumstances can change due to delayed house closings and other legitimate reasons for postponement.

Here is a good example of how you might be able to save money by getting the proper form signed well in advance of your actual moving date. For the past few years many of the major companies have increased transportation rates 10% during the summer months (June 1-September 30). Let's assume you do not know the exact day you want the truck to

47

load. If you think you may be moving in June or July (after the children are out of school), sign up with the company selected on the last day of May to "lock in" the guaranteed price for 60 days. In this situation, you should not have to pay the 10% seasonal rate increase if the truck is loaded during all of June and most of July (the last day of July will be past the 60-day allowance). If this is a likely time frame for your move, you may only want to entertain bids from companies which have a "company policy", as well as I.C.C.approval to guarantee prices for 60 days.

This one example can sometimes save hundreds of dollars if a move is being planned immediately after the kids get out of school. The same would apply just prior to any anticipated rate increase, anytime during the year. The importance of pre-planning a relocation and thoroughly following the methods outlined, cannot be stressed enough.

THE "BOTTOM-LINE" DISCOUNTED ESTIMATE

This type of estimate, as well as the "not to exceed" estimate (discussed in the following sub-section), are less frequently used compared to the Binding type. However, they each offer options that can sometimes be the appropriate way to go.

A huge benefit to the Binding estimate is that it can provide an exact price. This certainly allows your mind and bank account to rest comfortably during the entire relocation process. However, a "bottom-line" discounted estimate can *sometimes* result in a lower cost for the same services. The reason is simple. All of the additional charges (except storage related costs and liability coverage in some cases), are usually entitled to the same discount. The Binding estimate may exclude some of the "extras" from discounting. (With all of the options, the percentage of discount depends on the competitive nature of the companies in each community.)

With this type of estimate, the company is not guaranteeing an exact price for the move. What will be guaranteed is the "percentage of discount" applied to the company's tariff rates *for the actual weight and actual services provided* (excluding liability coverage and storage costs).

The truck will be weighed before arriving at the residence, and weighed a second time after loading. *The transportation rate in effect on the day the truck loads is what will be used as the base from which the percentage of discount will be deducted. The rates for other services will also be based on the tariff rates in effect on the day those services are provided.*

The final cost for the move can increase or decrease in accordance with the actual services provided, the exact weight of the household, as well as the number of boxes provided and/or packed by the company. Nothing is guaranteed except the "percentage of discount" that will be applied.

If an itemized estimate contains no additional charges, other than the cost for basic transportation, there is little benefit to receiving a "bottom-line" discounted estimate, compared to the Binding type which is discounted by the same percentage (unless you knew the actual weight of your shipment was going to be less than estimated).

Once the shipment is weighed, the driver will usually call to give notification of the amount due at destination. If the charges are higher than the total stated, you are required to pay up to 10% over the estimated total before the movers will begin unloading. The balance is due within 30 days.

With this type of estimate, a few circumstances can potentially develop, other than the shipment weighing more, which can result in an increase in cost. First, you must keep your fingers crossed so that no rate increase goes into effect between the time you receive the estimate and the time the truck actually loads. If the rates do increase, you are stuck paying more. (Don't hold your breath waiting for the rates to decrease!) Secondly, if the company changes its discount policy prior to loading, you may also encounter problems.

Remember, while the final cost can sometimes be lower, it can also be higher! For those who do not mind "flipping a coin" or "rolling the dice", this alternative may be preferred.

THE "NOT TO EXCEED" GUARANTEED ESTIMATE

This type of estimate is a combination of both the Binding and "bottom-line" discounted estimates. It is becoming increasingly more popular every day, since it provides an attractive alternative. It provides "peace of mind" in knowing the total charges are guaranteed "not to exceed" the estimated amount. Of course, this is assuming that no additional items are added and no other services are requested or needed after the estimate has been provided.

The estimate will state the "percentage of discount" which will be applied to the *actual* weight and other charges itemized on the estimate (except liability coverage and storage related costs.) *In addition, it will contain a total cost figure that is guaranteed "not to exceed" that amount.* Most companies will guarantee the total price for the same length of time as the Binding type. (Read sub-section "How Long Is The Price Guaranteed For?") Be sure to ask all representatives about their "company policy".

After the "percentage of discount" is applied, the total amount for all itemized services can potentially decrease. For instance, let's assume the total cost for a 5000-pound shipment, after a 20% discount, is guaranteed "not to exceed" $2,000. If the actual weight was only 4000 pounds, the transportation cost for the move would decrease after being calculated at that poundage. If the actual weight turned out to be 6000 pounds, you would not be required to pay more, unless items were added after the estimator took the room-by-room survey.

If you decide to add or delete items or services, make sure the estimator is informed long before moving day. Both the survey sheet and the estimate may need to be adjusted. In some cases, an "addendum" form can be utilized for minor changes.

The "not to exceed" estimate should not be overlooked, just because it is being explained last. It can often be the proper option to select, and should be discussed with each moving company along with the other options.

THE "TOO GOOD TO BE TRUE" BINDING ESTIMATE

The intent of deregulation was to create friendly competition and creativity among moving companies. It was supposed to provide the customer with better services, at reasonable prices. That goal has been reached. However, the industry is gradually becoming a wide-open "price war" where the "survival of the fittest" philosophy prevails.

Many of the experienced estimators have found other professions. The "cut-throat" atmosphere has made it difficult for many to adjust. The veterans are sometimes replaced by new salespeople whose training and expertise leave much to be desired.

Since you should have a feeling of confidence in the person you ultimately select, ask all representatives how many years they have been estimating. This is not to suggest you should disregard an estimate from a "rookie". Many companies have excellent training programs. Simply ask enough questions to ensure what is being promised is both accurate and complete. Irregardless of price, you do not want problems when the movers arrive on moving day. Misunderstandings should be resolved long before then, allowing adequate time to cancel an order-for-service and go with another company.

If you received three estimates for similar services to be performed in the $3,000 range, and one estimator guarantees the same services for $1500, BEWARE! Remember the old adage, "If it sounds too good to be true, it probably is!" An unscrupulous salesperson may call a few days before moving day to apologize for miscalculations or omissions on the estimate. Some may be honest mistakes, others somewhat doubtful. A representative is aware of the difficulty a person

51

will experience trying to switch to another company with last minute notification. Do not let mistakes or misunderstandings happen at the last minute. *If time allows, call the representative a few weeks beforehand to review all details.*

Remember, there is nothing obligating you to move with a particular company, until moving day when the Bill of Lading is signed. This is very important to keep in mind, especially if you receive a "bad news phone call" after signing an order-for - service.

In conclusion, be very cautious of any estimate that seems ridiculously low, compared to others. As a matter of fact, throw it out with yesterday's newspaper!

THE "BREAK-POINT"
(How You May Qualify To Have Extra Items Loaded *Without Additional Cost*)

Depending on the weight of your shipment, you may be entitled to add items without paying more than originally calculated in a Binding or "not to exceed" type of estimate. (If you received an estimate that allows the total cost to potentially go higher, it would be risky to add additional items.)

Whether or not you qualify, can only be answered by the person who provided the estimate. That person can make changes on all copies of the inventory which will avoid problems on moving day. In order to determine the transportation cost, the representative estimated the total weight of your shipment. After finding the correct mileage, the rate for each 100 pounds was determined. The rate *decreases at higher weight categories* (see example in Section 1, if you are confused). Therefore, if you have a little less weight than the next higher category, it is actually cheaper to figure the transportation cost by using the rate in the next higher category.

For example, if the estimator calculates there are 3800 pounds, the transportation cost will be figured at 4000 pounds. This will be done because it is cheaper. This is where the

"break-point" comes into play! Use the following example to learn the basic principle, but *remember the prices are fictitious.*
Example:

MILES	POUNDAGE	BREAK-POINT	POUNDAGE
261-280	2000-3999	(3600)	4000-7999
	$30		$27
	per 100 Lbs		per 100 Lbs

Let's assume the estimator figured your household goods weighed 3700 pounds. The rate for each 100 pounds using this example, would fall into the 2000-3999 pound category. The rate would be $30 for each 100 pounds. Therefore, your basic transportation cost would total $30 X 37 ($1110). The "break-point" is 3600 pounds. If you have between 3600 pounds and 4000 pounds, it is cheaper to calculate the cost at the rate in the 4000 pound category $27 x 40 ($1080). As you can readily observe, the total transportation cost becomes a lesser amount when the total poundage is over the "break-point", and is calculated at the next poundage category.

When the estimator is providing a Binding or "not to exceed" estimate, ask what was figured as the *actual* weight. In this example, you would be able to add an extra 400 pounds to your shipment, since you would be paying for 4000 pounds anyway! Remember the things you were thinking of discarding to minimize the cost? If a "break-point" is involved, you may be entitled to have the representative add certain items to all inventory sheets while not paying a dime more. Remember, it is never cheaper to transport more items, except where a "break-point" is involved. Therefore, start your weeding out process today!

SCHEDULING PICKUP AND DELIVERY

"What do you mean, I can't have everything loaded on Monday and delivered 2,000 miles away on Friday? I have driven that distance in 4 days, and besides, I thought your company has a fleet of professional drivers?" These comments are usually uttered by individuals who are unaware of the procedure involved when scheduling a long-distance move.

Complaints about moving companies are most frequently heard because of problems with delays. A better understanding of what the driver and the dispatcher must endure, may help to instill more patience and tolerance.

Each shipment is usually scheduled to load and/or unload in conjunction with others. A large van can transport three or more average-sized households. A delay at any of the scheduled pickups or deliveries can cause a "chain reaction" resulting in subsequent delays. For this reason, it is very difficult to arrange a day for loading or unloading, without providing the company with a few alternative days as an option. This is called a "spread". Unless there are extenuating circumstances beyond the company's control, it is obligated to perform the moving service within the agreed upon "spreads".

If you wanted your household goods to load on Wednesday, the company might ask for a "spread" of Wednesday through Friday. This would be considered a three-day "load spread". It doesn't help anyone's digestive tract, but it does provide the moving company with the flexibility needed to schedule other shipments on the same truck.

If a rather large shipment needs to be loaded, the company may agree on the exact weekday selected. (Read subsection entitled "Weekend Loading/Delivery", if weekend service is needed.) It may also agree to load on an exact day, if the shipment is in a community that has a steady flow of trucks passing through. It is easier to schedule a pickup in a large metropolitan area, since there are normally more trucks available. If the load is in a small town which is "off the beaten path", the company will need a "load spread" of at least two or three days. If the shipment is small (one or two rooms), even if it is located in a large city, expect as much as a week for a "load spread". It would be very unusual for a company to agree to load a small shipment within a one-or two-day period.

Unless a shipment occupies the entire space on a truck, it will probably be placed with other households. There may already be a few shipments on the truck when it arrives. If not,

Loading and Unloading – Can be performed by using large doors on the side of a moving van. This allows the movers to unload a shipment without moving others that were loaded afterwords.

there will usually be a few others scheduled to load after departing the residence. There are large doors on both sides of most moving vans that allow a shipment to be unloaded without disturbing other shipments loaded afterwards.

Each stop the driver makes as he winds his way down the highway, can often involve a full day of work. He is not always stopping for a sandwich and a cup of coffee. He may have to spend a full day loading or unloading another household. It is a very strenuous, time-consuming, and tiresome procedure. Since nobody wants one's possessions handled by fatigue-stricken movers, reasonable "delivery spreads" are given to every shipment. The length of time for delivery is much more complicated to predetermine than the loading schedule. Obviously, the number of miles the driver must travel is the most important factor. Also, the number of other shipments that must be serviced by the same truck is of equal importance. Poor weather and nasty traffic conditions can also cause scheduling problems. The "delivery spread" will take these factors, as well as others, into consideration.

Scheduling should be thoroughly discussed with each representative. The dates or "spread" should be reasonable, and acceptable to your situation. Make sure they are written on the order form, as well as the Bill of Lading which you must sign on moving day. Do not depend on a verbal promise, since it can potentially create misunderstanding.

When delays occur, the I.C.C. requires a company to notify the shipper by telephone, telegram, or in person. Therefore, do not have your telephone service disconnected prematurely. When an operating telephone is unavailable at the the new residence, the company should be given an alternate number to use for delivering a message (a neighbor, friend, relative, motel, place of employment, etc.). If the company is unable to deliver a message, it can hardly be criticized for not doing so. Always keep the "lines of communication" open.

The moving company may give you an E.T.A. (Estimated Time of Arrival). This is only an educated guess or "target day" within the agreed upon "delivery spread." Don't assume the day is "cast in cement"! Many things can happen between the time the driver departs and the time he is scheduled to deliver.

WEEKEND LOADING/DELIVERY
(How Overtime Charges Sometimes Can Be Avoided)

It is sometimes possible to have a shipment loaded or delivered on a Saturday or Sunday, without paying an additional cost for overtime labor. If you *specifically request* either day, you are required to pay extra. However, a "spread of days" can often be arranged with a company where the "spread" includes a Saturday or Sunday. If it is more convenient *for the company* to load or deliver on either day due to its scheduling of trucks, you are not obligated to pay extra.

For instance, if you prefer to move on Saturday, the representative may agree to set the "load spread" for Friday *and* Saturday. If the company has a truck to conveniently service your move on Saturday, you should not have to pay overtime labor for loading. In other words, you have given the company *the option of either day,* and it chose Saturday.

While a Friday/Saturday "load spread" option is fairly common, a Sunday/Monday load is not. Besides, it is not recommended to try loading on a Sunday since most offices are closed. The driver usually needs to pick up paperwork from the local agency. Even though he may be in town and anxious to perform the move, he cannot do anything without the necessary paperwork. While some offices may be closed on a Saturday, sometimes the driver can make prior arrangements to pick up the paperwork elsewhere. On a Sunday, it is very difficult to locate anyone.

Other problems can develop when trying to load on a weekend. The driver may need the local agent to provide additional helpers to load the truck. He may also need to obtain boxes from the local warehouse. On weekends, additional helpers and material may not be readily available to properly service a move. Even when the driver makes prior arrangements with the local agent, things can still get "botched up"! Therefore, try to avoid weekends. Do not think the problems discussed could never happen to you. If you are determined to move on a weekend, remember "I told you so"!

THE $100-$125 PER DAY, CASH REFUND PROGRAM FOR DELAYS

Wouldn't it be nice if your telephone company, carpet cleaning company, or other service company gave away large sums of money if they arrived late, or didn't show up at all? Well, guess what?? Some of the larger interstate moving companies will give cash reimbursements if they are unable to perform their service during the agreed upon schedule. (Note: read the very last "service" discussed in Section 9 to learn about an unbelieveable program offered by one company.)

These cash refunds are not received by individuals who happen to know someone important working for the company. They are programs that most people can qualify for. However, you must *specifically ask* to be placed on the program. It is not a "benefit" that everyone is automatically entitled to receive.

If a shipment is placed on this program, the shipper is entitled to receive a cash reimbursement for each day the truck is late for pickup and/or delivery. The company must perform within the "spread of days" that was agreed upon. Presently, some companies are giving $125 per day, while others are giving $100 per day. This is money that goes directly to the shipper, after promptly filing a "delay claim" with the company (should be filed within a month after delivery). *Even if an employer is paying for the relocation, you can personally receive this cash reimbursement.*

The agreed upon schedule is stated on both the order-for-service and the Bill of Lading. In addition, both forms should state that the shipment is moving "subject to the guaranteed pickup and delivery program". Companies that provide this program will usually have a small section on each of the two forms that can easily be completed before signing.

Even though the size of the shipment must qualify, it is not difficult to do so. Each company that provides this "benefit" has its own set of requirements. For instance, some companies may require the shipment to weigh at least 3500 pounds, while others may require the weight to be at least 5000 pounds. The time of the year when the move is to take place can sometimes be a factor in these minimum requirements. Some companies have a higher poundage minimum during the summer months, when scheduling is more difficult to arrange. However, even if the minimums needed to qualify are 3500 or 5000 pounds, one should keep in mind that the "average" room full of household goods will normally weigh 1000-1500 pounds. Therefore, it is not too difficult for a two-or three-bedroom household to qualify.

Some companies will not place a shipment on this program if it must be loaded from a storage facility at origin, or is being placed in storage at destination. Also, occasionally there are conditions beyond the company's control. These would include such occurrences as strikes, riots or natural disasters causing impassable road conditions.

When the company representative is providing the cost estimate, ask if it is possible to qualify for the "guaranteed pickup and delivery program". Not all interstate companies provide this "extra benefit", but some of the larger ones do. Ask each representative about any additional conditions the company may have.

LIABILITY COVERAGE

"Valuation protection" is provided on interstate moves to reimburse individuals for loss or damage caused by the mover. Since moving companies are not insurance carriers, and their representatives are not insurance salespeople, they are not normally selling a separate "insurance policy". In the moving industry, it is commonly called "released rate liability protection". There are a few options available that range in price from free to a few hundred dollars.

"Mrs. Jones, they're the exact same dishes, just shaped a little differently."

Before entering into any agreement to pay for extra liability protection, carefully review your homeowner's insurance policy. Some policies will cover loss or damage to household goods while being moved, and others will not. Call your insurance agent for a full explanation. If your policy does not presently provide this coverage, ask about the cost for a "temporary rider" that may be available.

It is important to fully understand the extent of liability the moving company will assume. There are a few choices from which to select whatever you feel most comfortable with. The selection you make *should be filled in and signed by you on the Bill of Lading (your contact with the moving company)*. Read it carefully to make sure the "valuation section" is accurate. If any catastrophe should occur, you and the moving company are legally bound by its terms.

THE "BASIC TYPE" (FREE)

At no extra cost, the mover's liability for loss or damage is limited to a maximum of 60 cents per pound per article, for the *actual weight of each lost or damaged article*. This is the basic, limited liability that is free-of-charge but *must be* specifically *ordered by you.* If this is your choice, you must write, in your own handwriting, in the valuation section on the Bill of Lading, "60 cents per pound per article". This is the bare minimum, provided at no charge, when you are *specifically waiving additional coverage.*

Because this type of coverage is tied to the weight of the item or items lost or damaged *instead of the actual value,* getting fairly reimbursed for any claim is close to impossible. For example, let's assume your great grandmother's antique clock is appraised at $600, and weighs 10 pounds. If it were totally destroyed beyond recognition, the maximum reimbursement for the clock would be 60 cents x 10 ($6). You can bet your great grandmother would be rolling over in her grave if she heard that one!

In conclusion, even though the "60 cents per pound per article" coverage is free, it usually does not fairly compensate for loss or damage caused by the moving company. Paying for additional coverage is highly recommended and is not very expensive.

DEPRECIATED VALUE PROTECTION
(Cost is $5 per $1000 of Declared Value)

With this type of coverage, the weight of an article is not important in determining fair compensation for loss or damage. It covers repairs, replacement or reimbursement at the item's *present value*. However, this figure is *based on depreciated value* using an adjusting process. For example, a $500 sofa purchased a few years ago may be worth only $200 today. Also, even if the sofa has been sitting in a living room for a year without being used, it probably started depreciating the moment it left the furniture store. Therefore, in requesting reimbursement for the present value of an item lost or damaged, don't expect the same amount you paid a few years ago. In this respect, it works similar to automobile insurance. If you just demolished a 1982 vehicle, you would hardly expect to be provided with a new one.

This type of additional protection can be purchased through the moving company at a cost of $5 per $1000 of declared value. (If you estimate the worth of your entire shipment at $20,000, the cost would be $5 x 20 or $100.) The I.C.C. has established a minimum amount that *must be declared* for the entire shipment to be released with this type of coverage. The minimum is calculated by multiplying the total weight of the shipment, times $1.25 for each pound. For instance, if your shipment weighed 4000 pounds, you would have to declare a total of *at least* $5,000 ($1.25 x 4000). You could declare a higher amount, but never lower.

The I.C.C. decided almost two decades ago, that the "average" worth of an "average" household could be approximated by using $1.25 per pound as a basis. This has never been updated to account for nearly 20 years of inflation! Today, the average family with a few children could hardly replace the contents of their closets for $5,000. Therefore, you should think twice before using $1.25 per pound as a basis for arriving at the total amount of coverage you declare. In most cases, it is simply inadequate to fairly compensate for a total loss. You should declare a "lump sum value" which is adequate to protect the true value of the shipment, just to be safe.

Failure to declare any value on the Bill of Lading automatically results in the shipment being valued at $1.25 x the total poundage. You are then obligated to pay $5 for each $1000 of value (50 cents per $100). Therefore, when signing the Bill of Lading, *if you do not want or need extra coverage, be sure to write "60 cents per pound per article" on the appropriate line.*

Example of a typical "valuation statement" on a Bill of Lading:

"UNLESS THE SHIPPER EXPRESSLY RELEASES THE SHIPMENT TO A VALUE NOT EXCEEDING 60 CENTS PER POUND PER ARTICLE, THE CARRIER'S MAXIMUM LIABILITY FOR LOSS OR DAMAGE SHALL BE EITHER THE LUMP SUM VALUE DECLARED BY THE SHIPPER OR AN AMOUNT EQUAL TO $1.25 TIMES THE ACTUAL WEIGHT IN POUNDS OF THE SHIPMENT, WHICHEVER IS GREATER."
The shipment will move subject to the rules and conditions of the carrier's tariff. Shipper hereby releases the entire shipment to a value not exceeding

$_____

(to be completed by person signing below)
NOTICE: THE SHIPPER SIGNING THIS CONTRACT MUST INSERT IN THE SPACE ABOVE, IN HIS/HER OWN HANDWRITING, EITHER THE DECLARATION OF THE ACTUAL VALUE OF THE SHIPMENT, OR THE WORDS "60 cents per pound per article". OTHERWISE THE SHIPMENT WILL BE DEEMED RELEASED TO A MINIMUM VALUE EQUAL TO $1.25 TIMES THE WEIGHT OF THE SHIPMENT IN POUNDS.

Shipper   Date

"Honeybuns, I can't remember which side of the bed is *my* side."

For further information concerning I.C.C. regulations regarding this subject, as well as others, ask the company representative for the I.C.C. publication entitled "Your Rights and Responsibilities When You Move". It is a free pamphlet you should find to be very informative.

FULL VALUE REPLACEMENT PROTECTION
(No Depreciation Figured In)

Let's assume you have come to the conclusion that "60 cents per pound per article" is a real joke. In addition, your household is full of items that cost a lot of money to purchase within the last couple of years. Or, you have collected an abundance of antiques that have not depreciated in value since their purchase. How do you get fairly compensated if damage or loss should occur?

Most of the larger companies now provide an option called Full Value protection. It protects the declared value of the entire household for the cost of repair or replacement, *without any reduction for depreciation.* This is the best protection available through interstate movers. Like most of the other options and services offered, this type of valuation coverage can vary between companies. Some have different minimum amounts that must be declared. One company may insist you declare a total of at least $15,000, while another may require a different minimum. With many companies, you must purchase an amount equal to at least $3.50 for each pound. For example, if a shipment weighs 10,000 pounds, at least $35,000 total valuation must be declared (10,000 x $3.50 = $35,000).

The price you pay for this type of coverage will also vary between companies. (Around $8.50 for each $1,000 of declared value.) For $35,000 worth of coverage, the cost would be 35 x $8.50 or $297.50 at that price.

Most companies that offer this type of protection also provide the same coverage with a "deductible". The price with a "deductible" will often be less than one half of the cost. You can obtain plans with a $300 deductible for $3.50 for each $1,000 of declared value. In the previous example, the cost for $35,000 worth of full value coverage was $297.50. If you are willing to absorb the first $300 of the total claim filed, the cost for the coverage would only be $122.50 (35 x $3.50). The difference in price is $175. In this case, this is money saved "up-front", providing you do not need to file a large claim. However, even if you did have a large claim, you would only be $125 "behind the 8 ball" since the $175 saved "up-front" is still in your bank account! The same principle would apply if the total value of your household was very high.

Example:

$100,000 of coverage with no deductible

$$(100 \times \$8.50) = \$850$$

$100,000 of coverage with $300 deductible

$$(100 \times \$3.50) = \underline{\$350}$$

Saved "up-front".. $500

NOTE: If you itemize your tax deductions, ask your tax advisor about "writing-off" a portion of the deductible amount if you file a claim.

Ask each company about the various options available. The rules, regulations and cost for the full value programs will vary. Educate yourself, so that your ultimate selection will provide "peace of mind".

FILING A CLAIM
(When Things Go Wrong)

Unfortunately, damage and/or loss are "facts of life" when household goods are transported. They are simply not manufactured to endure the constant stress of being moved on and off of trucks. If you attempt this task yourself, you may have sawdust to sweep up. If the professionals make a mistake, you have someone to blame; someone to collect money from; and someone to do the sweeping for you.

On occasion, if the amount of damage or loss is small (less than $100), the movers may "cough up" the money out of their own pockets. Since they do not like giving money away, they would only consider doing so if it was obvious they were at fault. In general, they do not relish having an abundance of small claims blemish their performance record.

If a claim needs to be filed, the mover's liability will depend on the type of protection you selected and wrote on the Bill of Lading. It is *your responsibility* to obtain the necessary claim forms from the moving company. Unless the company has a toll-free telephone number, call the closest agent for the company that moved you. They usually cooperate with each other when claims occur, but all settlements are usually processed through the company's main headquarters. "Blowing off steam" with the local office is a waste of time.

When communicating with the company's main office, always refer to your "order-for-service" number, which can be found on the upper corner of the Bill of Lading. Today, everything is computerized to provide fast and efficient services. This number is what the company plugs into its computer system.

Sometimes damage can occur while the truck is being loaded. If so, make notations on your copy of the inventory sheet, as well as the mover's copy. This will be important evidence to support your claim in the future. However, do not expect the movers or the company to negotiate a settlement until after the move has been paid for, and you have submitted the necessary claim forms. Remember, the movers will not unload at destination until they are paid, unless other arrangements were previously made. If an employer is paying for the relocation, claims will usually not be processed until the company pays the total amount due.

While waiting for the claim forms to be sent, and during the entire process, nothing should be done with the damaged items. *The company expects an opportunity to respond, and possibly view the damage.* It may want to send a repairman, refinisher or appraiser to the residence for an inspection.

Remember, the moving company is allowed to restore an item to its condition when it was loaded on the truck. It may choose to have this done, instead of reimbursing you.

After making notations on all copies of the inventory sheets describing damage and/or loss, you will be asked to sign each one. You will also be asked to sign the Bill of Lading. In doing so, you are agreeing to accept your shipment in *apparent* good condition, except for damage or loss that has been noted. It is a good idea to write on the Bill of Lading "subject to final inspection of all items for concealed damage or loss". If you should discover that an article was lost or damaged after accepting delivery, you are still entitled to file a claim even though notations were not placed on the inventory sheets. However, your notations *help support your claim*.

I.C.C. regulations allow you to file a claim with a moving company *within 9 months* after accepting delivery. This period allows ample time to discover "concealed" damage. However, promptly filing a claim is highly recommended.

Inspect the boxes containing fragile items and those that appear crushed or dented, as soon as possible. If time allows, you should do so while the movers are still unloading the truck. The longer you wait to discover "concealed" damage, the harder it will be to prove the movers were responsible. If broken items are discovered in boxes, leave them in the same boxes for the company to inspect. Remember, it is your responsibility to furnish "reasonable proof" of the mover's liability.

If the moving company packs a box, it will normally accept responsibility for damage to its contents. If damage is immediately discovered, either the box was mishandled or the contents were packed "improperly".

If you pack the containers yourself, proving the mover's liability for "concealed" damage is always a "gray area". If a box you packed is delivered looking like an accordion, there is a good chance it was improperly placed inside the truck. However, if the exterior of the carton looks perfect, and you did not observe it being dropped or mishandled, it may be hard to prove you packed the box "properly". This "gray area" is frequently a source of controversy. Some companies make it very difficult to collect "concealed" damage claims for boxes they did not pack.

The movers have the right to inspect cartons before assuming responsibility. If they feel any box is not packed properly, they can ask you to repack it. If you refuse to do so, they do not have to load it on the truck unless you write on the inventory sheet "moving company is not liable for damage to contents of box #" ... Remember, they do not want damage anymore than you do.

If you have any flammable, explosive, or pressurized items (aerosol cans, paint, bullets, tank of propane, etc.), do not include them in the shipment. These items are dangerous to put on a truck. Moving vans do not have windows for ventilation, and often get extremely hot inside. Should anything of this nature cause damage, do not expect the moving company to honor your claim. It is not responsible for an act or omission on your part. Also, no company will assume liability for an inherent vice or defect of an article, from acts of God, war-like or hostile action, etc. What it boils down to is, "if you can prove it is their fault, you win; but if you or anyone else is to blame, you lose!"

Moving companies do not allow a shipment of household goods to contain high-valued items such as coin or stamp collections, valuable documents, expensive jewelry, cash, etc. Therefore, items of this nature should be transported separately. You will have a hard time filing a claim for a missing box containing your life's savings or your $20,000 stamp collection.

Winning a claim for other missing items of high value will also be difficult if you do not have some sort of iron-clad evidence. If a box contains a $500 antique vase, it would be smart to take a photograph and have an appraisal made prior to placing it in a box. A recent purchase receipt would also help to substantiate a future claim. Also, when transporting any item of special value, mark on the box or article *and on the inventory sheets* (driver's copy and your copy), "item # ... valued at ..."

Once the claim forms are completed and submitted to the company, it is required by the I.C.C. to give written acknowledgement within 30 days after receipt. Within 120 days after receipt, it is required to either pay, deny, or make a compromise settlement. If the company is unable to do so, it is required to give you a written explanation every 30 days thereafter explaining the reason for delay. If the moving company is not following these guidelines, complain to the I.C.C. office closest to your new home. (A list of office locations follow later in this section.)

Loss and/or damage claims are not resolved by the I.C.C. It does not have the authority to force a settlement. Its function is to enforce rules and regulations. You should write to the I.C.C. only if you feel the company has not properly responded to your claim; or has violated its contract (obligations stated in the Bill of Lading); or has violated some I.C.C. rules.

When unable to settle your claim with a company, you may file a civil action by going to court. However, it can often be expensive and time consuming. This avenue should only be used as a last resort.

There is another course of action, sometimes available, that can be quicker and cheaper than a courtroom. With many of the larger companies, as long as both parties agree, your claim can be submitted to an "arbitrator" who works for an independent agency called the American Arbitration Association. Even though this agency is sponsored by the American Movers Conference, the "dispute settlement program" acts as a neutral observer. It is an independent, non-governmental organization which is not directly affiliated with the moving companies.

Not all companies use an arbitration program. Ask each representative about this. Further information can be found in the free pamphlet written by the I.C.C. ("Your Rights And Responsibilities When You Move").

INTERSTATE COMMERCE COMMISSION
OFFICE LOCATIONS

Throughout the country, the I.C.C. has "field offices" to assist the consumer. It has the responsibility of maintaining a safe and efficient system for all types of interstate transportation. If there is a complaint or grievance of any kind, the I.C.C. wants to know about it. Also, if you would like to express satisfaction with the manner in which your move was serviced, the I.C.C. would not be adverse to receiving a complimentary letter. It even provides a "postage paid" card on the back of its free pamphlet for your convenience.

ARIZONA

2028 Federal Bldg.
230 North First Ave.
Phoenix, 85025

CALIFORNIA

1321 Federal Bldg.
300 North Los Angeles St.
Los Angeles, 90012

211 Main St.
Suite 500
San Francisco, 94105

COLORADO

142 U.S. Customs House
721-19th St.
Denver, 80202

FLORIDA

4057 Carmichael Ave.
Suite 233
Jacksonville, 32207

INDIANA

Federal Bldg.
46 East Ohio St.
Room 429
Indianapolis, 46204

LOUISIANA

T-9038 Federal Bldg.
701 Loyola Ave.
New Orleans, 70113

MARYLAND

1025 Federal Bldg.
Charles Center
31 Hopkins Plaza
Baltimore, 21201

MASSACHUSETTS

150 Causeway St.
Room 501
Boston, 02114

GEORGIA

Peachtree Twenty-Fifth Bldg.
1718 Peachtree St., N.W.
Suite 360
Atlanta, 30309

ILLINOIS

Everett McKinley Dirksen Bldg
219 South Dearborn St.
Room 1304
Chicago, 60604

NEBRASKA

Federal Bldg.
106 South 15th St.
Room 728
Omaha, 68102

NEW YORK

Jacob K. Javits Federal Bldg.
26 Federal Plaza
Room 1807
New York City, 10278

NORTH CAROLINA

Mart Office Bldg.
800 Briar Creek Road
Room CC-516
Charlotte, 28205

OHIO

Celebrezze Federal Bldg.
1240 East 9th St.
Room 913
Cleveland, 44119

MINNESOTA

Federal Bldg.
110 South Fourth St.
Room 475
Minneapolis, 55401

MISSOURI

2111 Federal Bldg
911 Walnut St.
Kansas City, 64106

PENNSYLVANIA

3535 Market St.
Room 16400
Philadelphia, 19104

TEXAS

411 West 7th St.
Suite 500
Fort Worth, 76102

UTAH

2419 Federal Bldg.
125 State St.
Salt Lake City, 84138

WASHINGTON

858 Federal Bldg.
915 Second Ave.
Seattle, 98174

SECTION 5

UNLOADING AT DESTINATION

"Now that I paid to move all this ..., where am I going to put it ?"
- Janet, after moving from a three bedroom house to a
one bedroom apartment.

When the truck arrives at the new residence, you must pay before the unloading begins (unless previous arrangements were made). Personal checks are rarely accepted by any company. Many people get insulted when they hear this. However, it is simply too easy to "get burned" in the moving industry when people are usually closing bank accounts. It is not good business practice to provide a service to someone who is 1000 miles away, then discover two weeks later the check "bounced like a rubber ball". It is difficult for a company to collect after people are "snug as a bug in a rug" in their new home.

The driver will accept a certified check, money order, travelers checks or cash. I do not recommend paying with cash since you will be traveling with a large sum of money that other people would also like to be traveling with. Don't take the chance of getting "ripped-off". Travelers checks are a pain to use for this purpose, since you are stuck having to place your signature on numerous checks. A certified check is recommended for convenience and safety. As you are closing bank accounts before leaving town, have one drawn for the exact amount of the Binding price. If you received an estimate that could increase in price, have extra cash on hand. If you received one that can potentially decrease, the company should promptly send a refund check to the new address.

A few companies will accept charge cards if previous arrangements have been made. While the I.C.C. does allow their use, most companies have chosen not to accept them. Therefore, ask each representative about their usage if this is important to you. For most situations, a certified check is the proper way to go. (See Section 9 to learn about one company that has its own "credit plan".)

Once you arrive at the new residence, start preparing for the truck's arrival. Vacuum each room before the furniture arrives. Hopefully, you will be able to transport a vacuum cleaner in your automobile. If you do not have room in the car and need to place it on the truck, ask the movers to load it last. When they arrive at destination, it will be one the first things unloaded when the door opens. If one can be borrowed from a friend, neighbor or relative without having to promise "your first-born child" in return, that would be preferable. You should get this chore out of the way before the truck arrives.

Decide where the larger items will be positioned in each room. Determine the most appropriate placement for the bedroom set, sofa, bookcase, piano, etc. Try to visualize the best direction for the beds to face, and where the dressers will be most conveniently located. Discuss which child will be placed in the larger bedroom, and which child gets the little cubicle. Don't expect the movers to lend their aesthetic criticism or advice. They want to be given instructions *once*! Even the most patient of professional movers will become irate if they must reorganize a room to accommodate your changing whims. For this reason, draw a small sketch with a proposed floor plan for each room. It will help your recollection of what was pre-determined collectively by all family members. A plan will lessen the confusion and argumentation which usually develops during this procedure. It may also prevent your throat from getting inflamed!

The following scenario is what you want to avoid while the movers are holding your heavy sofa -"Honeybuns, I think I like it over here, what do you think?" "Well dearest sweet cheeks, let's try it over in that corner". "Then again, maybe it would be more suitable in the family room!" To avoid this dialogue, put your heads together before the movers arrive. It will minimize the chaos which is inherent when moving into a new environment. Since the driver may need to deliver another shipment 400 miles away on the next day, he will appreciate an organized and efficient unloading process. Time is money to him!

Once the driver is paid, the huge doors on the van will swing open and the unloading operation will commence. You will immediately notice that Mr. and Mrs. Busybody (your new neighbors) will be peeking through their curtains to check out the quality of your furniture. They will be forming their very first impressions. Ignore everything and everybody. Attend to the business of properly unloading your possessions. Take your shoes off and replace them with sneakers.

There are numerous things that need to be done to *properly* unload and place furniture where it belongs. Plan on working with the movers, from beginning to end, so you do not have to move heavy furniture yourself after they depart!

When the movers begin to unload, it is your responsibility to "check-off" the numbers on your inventory sheets. As you are doing so, look at each item for damage that did not previously exist. I recommend at least two people be present during the unloading. One should be outside to check the inventory sheets and the condition of everything being unloaded. The second person should be indoors, instructing the movers regarding the proper placement in each room. *If any damage is observed, make a notation on your copy of the inventory, as well as the driver's copy.* If you notice a box has been crushed or has a corner dented, inspect it immediately. If there is damage to the contents, make a note on your inventory sheet and driver's copy stating "box # _____ was received with contents damaged".

After unloading, the driver will expect you to sign his copy of the inventory. In doing so, you are stating you received

"I've got everything inside under control, honey!"

all items listed, and in the condition noted on the inventory. *Do not sign until you are certain all inventory numbers have been checked-off, and proper notations have been placed on all inventory sheets regarding damage you may have noticed.* This is extremely important since these sheets will be used by the claims department of the company should you file a claim in the future.

If you requested unpacking of boxes, direct the movers to those boxes once everything is situated in its proper place. Even though it is not very expensive to have boxes unpacked, *even for free,* I do not recommend having too much done! It is confusing to have everything taken out of boxes at a time when you are not sure what you want placed in certain locations. The usual result is a house that immediately becomes a total mess! Once everything is pulled out of boxes, the contents are usually spread on the floors, counter-tops and tables. You have no idea of what a monster this procedure can create, unless you have experienced it.

Do most of the unpacking in the leisurely days and weeks that follow. Don't try to accomplish too much on the day your possessions arrive. There may be a few items you do want unpacked by the movers and added into the price. Mattress and wardrobe boxes, mirrors, lamps and lamp shades are likely candidates. Because mattress and wardrobe boxes are bulky, it is wise to have the movers unpack and cart them away in their truck. If you put them at the curb on garbage day, the trashman is certain to scream obscenities if they are not cut and tied in small bundles. You may desire to keep the wardrobe boxes for storage of seasonal clothing. They can be sealed and placed in a garage or attic area with some mothballs inside. They are convenient, especially if you have limited closet space in the residence. You might request the unpacking of lamp bases and shades, as well as mirrors, since there is always an immediate need for these items. Lamps can be returned to their original table tops, and mirrors can be reattached to dressers. *All of this can easily be done by you.*

Do not expect the movers to be nice guys who will take your boxspring and mattress out of a box for free. They will probably reassemble the bedframe and lean the boxspring and mattress against a wall in the proper room. If they must unpack these boxes, they are entitled to a small labor charge for their effort. (One exception to this is explained in Section 9–Bekins' First Day Service.) While the majority of professional movers are nice guys, they don't believe in doing extra work for free. In conclusion, if you want any unpacking performed, have the estimator add the additional cost to the total price. Otherwise, nothing will come out of a box unless your movers are angels, and there doesn't seem to be any angels walking on earth.

When the unpacking is finished and the entire move has been completed, the necessary paperwork must be signed. After signing the inventory sheets and the Bill of Lading, you have essentially given the movers a receipt for your belongings. At that point, they will bid you farewell and ride off into a sunset or blizzard.

TIPPING

Should you give the driver and his helpers a tip, and what should the amount be? Only you can ultimately make this decision. I suggest you treat the situation as though you just finished dinner in a nice restaurant. The amount given to the waitress or waiter is proportional to the quality of service received. I am not suggesting you give a 15-20% tip or any amount that is proportionate to your moving bill. A small sum of money to the driver ($20 or so), and a smaller amount to his helpers ($10) is a nice "thank you".

While tipping is always an optional item, by all means reward the person who pampers your possessions at origin, and again upon completion of the move. If you have received good service and courteous treatment, recognize it and reward it!

"Thank you. We'll have to do this again sometime."

NOTES:

SECTION 6

THE EXTRAS

"It seems like I have spent one half of my life making arrangements to put my things into storage facilities, and the other half trying to figure out where to put everything afterwards."
   – Lou, a retired marine who needed storage at least ten times for his collection of four wheelbarrels, ten shovels, and numerous other unneeded "collectibles."

You may need services provided which are not included in the transportation cost. Expect extra charges for each service. A company will also charge more if certain conditions related to the move are not within the realm of "ordinary". In addition, there may be extra "handling charges" for items not in a "normal" shipment of household goods. All of the extra costs are outlined in each company's rate book (tariff). With the exception of packing labor costs, boxes, and unpacking costs, they are non-negotiable. (There are two big exceptions to this which are outlined in sub-sections entitled Bottom-Line and Not To Exceed Discounted Estimates.) The prices for some of these "extras" can vary between companies and counties. While the cost is not enormous, you can expect a small amount to be added into the estimate.

Each extra charge should be itemized on the estimate. Any service or "condition" needed at the new residence must be explained to the representative when calculating the total. *Do not attempt to conceal or avoid discussion of circumstances that may develop at the new residence, simply because you want to avoid paying more money.* If everything is not itemized on the estimate and added into the total price, no "extras" will be done unless you sign an "addendum". This form states you will pay the extra costs involved (see sub-section on "Addendums"). Nobody like surprises, especially a truck driver who arrives at a residence to discover he must deliver household goods to the fourth floor of a building which does not have an elevator. If he must accomplish this task, you can surely expect he wants to be fairly compensated for his extra efforts. Therefore, do not be evasive concerning little details at destination. The last thing you need is irate movers unloading your delicate items.

The "extras" have been divided into three categories: Special Conditions; Special "Handling" Charges; and Extra Services/Labor. While other charges can occur under unusual circumstances, the following is an explanation of the most common ones. *Use all of the prices stated as a guide. Prices will vary between companies, counties, and are subject to change.* The same is true for the regulations which relate to all of the following. Remember, this is only a guideline!

THE THREE SPECIAL CONDITIONS

There are three "conditions" that may exist when moving out of your present residence or into the new home. If any of these exist, expect a small additional charge. All three will be calculated into the total cost, based on the weight of the household goods. Some companies have a small minimum charge.

    1. The "Stair Carry"
       (approximately $.65-$1.00 for each 100 pounds)

"I hope I get there by tomorrow morning!"

There will be a charge if the movers must use 8 steps or more at a residence located on any floor other than the ground floor. Each additional flight is defined as the number of complete floors above or below the first flight. You should not be charged for a "stair carry" inside a single-family home. If furniture (except for a piano, organ or harpsichord) must be removed or placed on any floor of a single-family dwelling, it is considered "normal" and is the exception to the rule.

When the pickup or delivery involves stairs *outside any house or building,* you will be assessed in a similar fashion:

    8 to 27 steps = one "stair carry"
    28 to 47 steps = two
    48 to 67 steps = three
    68 to 87 steps = four
    88 to 107 steps = five
    each additional 20 steps or fraction thereof =
    additional flight

2. The "Excessive Distance Carry"
    (approximately $.65-$1.00 for each 100 pounds)

If the driver is unable to safely park the truck within a normal distance of your entrance (within 75 feet), you will be charged an "excessive distance carry". If you live in an apartment building, there will be a distance charge for any travel within the building which exceeds the 75 feet allowed. Each additional 50 feet or fraction thereof, constitutes an additional charge for another "distance carry".

3. The "Elevator Carry"
    (approximately $1.15-$1.45 for each 100 pounds)

When loading or delivery involves use of an elevator, you will be charged for an "elevator carry". (The only exception is when the elevator is in a single-family home.) The floor where an apartment or a condominium is located does not make any difference. When inside stairs and an elevator are both available, you should be charged using the least costly method.

"Don't worry, just start jumping up and down. If the cable breaks, we have a 50/50 chance of being in the air when it hits the bottom."

If an elevator needs to be utilized, make prior arrangements with the manager of the building. Be certain the elevator will definitely be available on the day of your move.

NOTE: When an automobile is figured in the total weight, the weight of the car should be deducted from the total before any of these "three special conditions" are calculated.

THE SPECIAL "HANDLING" CHARGES

You may have an item to be moved which is not considered part of a "normal" shipment of household goods. If you have any of the following, expect to pay a special "handling" charge. The list contains the most common items. (The cost figures provided are approximations.)

Automobile... $93
Motorcycle (250cc or over)............................ $58
Grandfather Clock (under 5 feet) $23
Grandfather Clock (over 5 feet) $41
Trailers (including utility and pop-up)................. $53
Campers (unmounted on trucks)...................... $134
Tool Sheds, Utility Sheds............................... $88
Playhouses (more than 100 cu.Ft.) $88
Spa, Hot-Tub, Whirlpool Bath $88
Jacuzzi (more than 100 cu.ft.) $88
Riding Mowers and Tractors
(25 horsepower and above) $70
Riding Mowers and Tractors
(less than 25 horsepower) $47
Snowmobiles and Riding Golf Carts $47
Farm Equipment, Implements
(more than 100 cu.ft.) $146
* Piano, Organ or Harpsichord
(over 38 inches in height)............................. $59*
Piano, Organ or Harpsichord
(38 inches or less) $25

*The special "handling" charge for a piano, organ or harpsichord is in addition to a separate charge for a "stair carry" that may be necessary, and not already figured in the estimate.

BULKY ARTICLES

If your shipment includes a "bulky article", expect to pay more for the excessive space occupied on the truck. The following group of items fall into this category. The estimator will measure the item to determine how much poundage should be added to the total weight. This is called a "weight additive". *The poundage is in addition to the actual weight of the article.*(This does not apply to boats, sailboats, skiffs, rowboats or kayaks that are less than 14 feet in length.)

Boats (14 feet and over in length)
- 115 pounds per linear foot of total length

Sailboats (14 feet and over in length)
- 125 pounds per linear foot of total length

Canoes, Kayaks, Skiffs, Light Rowboats
(14 feet and over in length)
- 40 pounds per linear foot of total length

Boat Trailers (any length)
- 75 pounds per linear foot of total length

Travel Campers, Trailers, Mini-Mobile Homes
(other than utility and pop-up trailers)
- 300 pounds per linear foot of total length

EXTRA SERVICES AND LABOR CHARGES

On a typical relocation, the basic transportation cost includes loading and unloading. The movers should place all furniture and boxes in each room requested. They should also disassemble regular bedframes and reassemble at destination. However, if the movers must perform tasks requiring additional labor at origin or destination, expect a small additional charge. For instance, if a waterbed must be disassembled at origin and/or reassembled at the new residence, expect most companies to add a labor charge (hourly rate). Most of the rates vary from county to county.

"I don't know if we still have room for the vacuum cleaner!"

Other examples would be outdoor swing sets or storage sheds that need disassembling and/or reassembling. Discuss the cost with the estimator when the total is being calculated. These items should be dismantled which can easily be done with "a little help from a friend". Do not assume the movers will perform these extra tasks unless they are paid for their labor.

If you *specifically request* labor performed between 5:00 p.m. and 8:00 a.m., overtime labor rates will apply. This is also true if you *specifically request* labor performed on Saturdays, Sundays or Holidays. Therefore, try to avoid these circumstances.

EXTRA PICKUP OR DELIVERY

There may be large items which need to be included in a shipment, but are not at the residence. Small things do not present a problem, since they can usually be transported in an automobile. However, what does one do when Aunt Lucy's antique piano is sitting in her garage 10 blocks away? Or, what about the bedroom set received as a wedding gift, but the furniture store is asking $100 to deliver? Or, there is the public storage unit that was rented to stuff all those unneeded things that wouldn't fit into your present residence.

The truck that is scheduled to come to your house can also make a stop before or after loading at your residence. This would need to be arranged and calculated into the total cost. Discuss your situation when the representative provides the estimate. While it is not very expensive (approximately $50 for each stop), the mileage between stops will be added to the total miles. If that total makes it necessary to calculate in a higher mileage category, the result will be a slightly higher transportation cost. Ask the representative if the distance between your residence and the extra stop will affect the "rate". If it does increase, the amount should be small.

If you decide to have the moving company perform any extra stops, find out what mileage limitations they may have.

There is a limit to the number of miles the movers will travel to accomplish this extra service. If it is a reasonable distance or "en route", there should be no problem. However, if you are moving from Los Angeles to New York City and have an extra pickup in Oregon, you can obviously forget it!

"THIRD PARTY" SERVICES

This type of service is needed for items requiring special treatment at origin and/or destination. *It is a special service provided by a different company.* The moving company can be a good source of information to locate qualified people to perform these services. It can usually make the necessary arrangements for you, but will probably add a small charge to do so. Get the name of qualified people to call, and save the cost of whatever commission the moving company may tack on. Besides, most moving companies do not like to get involved in this separate billing procedure.

Washer/Dryer –In order to transport a washer, the water hoses must be disconnected. There is also a styrofoam "washer block" available to place inside the machine to keep the agitator secured. These blocks can be purchased from most moving companies.

If you do not want to disconnect the water hoses and/or reconnect at destination, the moving company can make arrangements for a "third party" company to perform this easy task. If you want to make your own arrangements, just get the name of a "specialist" within the area. The same appliance specialist can also service a gas dryer which needs to be disconnected from the gas outlet.

Washer and dryer disconnections are not difficult. Each can easily be done with a pair of pliers. The local hardware store will have a small metal cap to screw on the gas outlet protruding from the wall.

Most movers do not want to perform this work because of a potential liability problem. If the water faucets are not closed properly or are defective, the water damage could be costly. If the gas shut-off valve is not closed properly and a leak develops, an explosion could occur. The movers do not want to accept responsibility for either situation. The probability of a problem occurring is small. However, legal problems have occurred in the past to discourage movers from being overly accommodating in this department. Their insurance rates are excessive because of the high risk nature of the business. The last thing they need is to have their coverage quadrupled or even dropped as a result of a major claim due to disconnecting a washer or dryer.

Pool Tables – If you have a small pool table, you can probably get by with taking the legs off. If you need to move a full-sized table with large pieces of slate, special servicing is usually required. The table should be disassembled with the slate placed in wooden crates. Your mover should be able to provide the name of a specialty company to do this. Companies that sell pool tables can also provide this information. When the time comes for reassembly in your new home, the Yellow Pages can be used to locate another company. A better idea would be to call the local agency of the company that moved you. It can provide valuable information. Ask for recommendations for whatever services are required. This will take the guesswork out of selecting a reputable company with reasonable prices.

Grandfather Clocks – If you have a grandfather clock with a pendulum and weights, they need to be placed in a box. If the clock has a complicated timing mechanism, a clock specialist should be used to disassemble and reassemble at destination. If the outer part of your clock is antique or somewhat fragile, the moving company can construct a wooden crate. Ask the estimator to measure and calculate the cost into the estimate.

The movers will construct and place the clock in a wooden crate, but they don't like to get involved in disassembly of the timing mechanism. These are precision items that should be handled by a specialist. They are specialists in moving! Do not expect them to be "jacks of all trades". Besides, some of them have hands that would never fit into Aunt Gertrude's antique clock!

"Mrs. Jones, I may need your assistance!"

TRANSPORTING PLANTS

Placing potted plants in the same van with household goods can be expensive. When you are paying for transportation on a poundage basis, dirt is expensive to move since it can be very heavy. One potted plant can sometimes weigh 50 pounds or more. When you consider the cost for each 100 pounds being moved, it is often cheaper and less risky to buy healthy ones later on.

Even if you are willing to pay to transport plants that have been "members of the family" for 10 years, no company will guarantee their survival. You may be doing those "prized possessions" a big favor by finding another happy home where they can flourish. Also, if you sell the "babies", that revenue can be used to purchase a new family at the other end. Bidding farewell to loved ones is always a difficult task.

Some states have restrictions that prohibit certain types of plants from entering. Others will allow entry if they have been already certified by state or federal pest control officials. You will have to call or write to the appropriate agricultural agency for the state you are moving into. Many states have brochures to send in response to inquiries. Before making a long-distance call, first try the county office of the State Department of Agriculture.

The prohibition is enforced to prevent nasty little bugs from infesting or contaminating the land. A few states are so concerned that they do not allow any plants to enter. Some allow certain plants, only if proof is available to show they have been properly sprayed.

If you are still reading about how to transport your plants, one might assume that you have not been totally discouraged yet. However, there is one more "whammo" involved in the process. *The movers cannot be forced to load them on the truck.* It is sort of the "driver's discretion". *If he feels your plants may infest his van, he has the right to refuse to load them.* He does not want bugs in his truck, anymore than you want them in your new home. Also, I.C.C. regulations state that the driver is not supposed to load plants in a van if traveling more than 150 miles or longer than 24 hours.

In conclusion, if you are willing to pay the price; endure the bureaucratic red tape; and take a gamble on the driver; your loyalty and persistence should be commended. However, the results of the "ultimate gamble" will not be known until your plants finally arrive at destination, alive.

If you are able to place a few of your most "loyal buddies" in the car, never put them in the trunk. Any extreme temperature changes can be disastrous. Water them a day before leaving and securely place in a cardboard box. Use newspaper to prevent the pots from moving, and be sure to line the box with a plastic trashbag beforehand. You do not want water seepage to ruin the cardboard and car seat. Do not over-water the plants before leaving, since you can always find water at "pit-stops".

Once your plants reach destination, place them in an environment they are accustomed to. Try to duplicate the same amount of light and shade which nurtured them in the past.

TRANSPORTING PETS

Since the movers will not place "Fee-Fee" in the truck, special arrangements will need to be made. The moving company should be able to provide the name of a "pet transportation" company if you do not want to take "Fee-Fee" with you. No matter what method is chosen, be sure to discuss with your veterinarian, any special requirements and precautions that must be considered. Many states require interstate health certificates and entry permits.

Requirements vary from one state to another. Most require rabies immunization and licensing for dogs. Some states also require that cats be licensed. Your local humane society or kennel can be a good source of information. If the veterinarian has a medical file for your pet, you may want to have that information forwarded to a veterinarian in your new community. Ask for a referral or recommendation.

When traveling by automobile, use a pet carrier or crate in the back seat. You do not need "Fee-Fee" jumping around, disturbing your concentration. To help your pet adjust before the trip, place the food and water bowl inside the container with the door constantly open. Give your pet ample time to adjust to the temporary quarters. To help it get accustomed to automobile transportation, a few short rides before the trip will be helpful.

While traveling, exercise your pet at the reststops. Always place a leash on the collar when doing so. New surroundings, curiosity, and normal nervousness can cause it to scamper away. You do not need unnecessary delays. If you must leave your pet in the car, avoid parking in the hot sun and be sure to leave the windows open a few inches.

Many airlines will transport pets if certain requirements are met. Size and construction of the container is important. They will not be overjoyed to see "Fee-Fee's" huge doghouse on the conveyor belt. Since most airlines limit baggage department space for pet transportation, make a reservation early.

No matter what method is used for transportation, sedation is sometimes required. Always consult a veterinarian before tranquilizing any pet.

TRANSPORTING AUTOMOBILES

If you are not overjoyed with the idea of driving your car on a long trip, there are a few options available to ease the burden. It is not a cheap service to arrange, but it can be a convenient luxury for those willing to pay the price.

One convenient method is to have the car loaded on the same truck with the household goods. Car ramps are utilized for this procedure. Once the vehicle is in position, tension straps are used to firmly hold down the suspension system. A platform is usually constructed over the car enabling the space above to be used for household goods.

It is not safe to place any items in the area surrounding the car. Also, it is not safe to pack the inside of the car with items that can be jostled around everytime the truck drives over a bump. Car seats can quickly transform into trampolines. This method is very convenient since everything can usually be loaded and delivered on one day at each end.

Another method which can often be less expensive is by using a "car carrier" truck. This is the type of vehicle used by car manufacturers when delivering new cars to a dealership. Many of the larger companies that transport household goods also have a fleet of "car carriers". While it is sometimes less expensive than placing a car on a moving van, you can usually expect a little inconvenience. There is a good chance the "car carrier" and the moving van will not load and/or deliver on the same day. Each vehicle will probably have a different schedule. If you don't mind waiting a few days for your car to arrive, the "car carrier" may be preferred. If you do not have an immediate need for the vehicle prior to departure, it is definitely worth considering. This is especially true if you must rent a car at your new location. However, since the "car carrier" may arrive at destination before you (if you are driving another vehicle), you may need to make arrangements for someone else to accept delivery and pay the driver. If you have more than one car to transport, the "car carrier" method is highly recommended. You will pay a fixed price (depending on mileage) for the first car. The cost for each additional car goes down when loaded as one shipment. The weight of a car is irrelevant when the "car carrier" method is used.

There are companies that specialize in automobile transportation (some even use railroad cars), and never handle household goods. If you are considering the use of a "car carrier", you can probably save money by making separate arrangements. They are usually cheaper than a company which specializes in household goods transportation. The names of these companies can be found in the Yellow Pages, or in the classified section of your newspaper.

Car Carrier – Vehicle used exclusively for automobile transportation.

After learning how much it will cost to transport your car, you may feel it is too expensive. There is an inexpensive alternative which can be used, but there is some risk involved. "Auto Drive-Away" agencies are located throughout the country which make arrangements to have people (often college students) drive the car for you. The problem is that you never know the driving record of the individual you have entrusted with the car. If you are willing to pay a few hundred dollars, and take the gamble, this option may be for you. These companies are listed in the Yellow Pages under "Auto Transporters", or in the classified section of the newspaper.

Another method would be to tow one car behind another you are driving. However, since a car can easily weigh over 2500 pounds, you had better be sure the vehicle that must pull the weight, is capable of doing so. Pulling over a ton of metal, especially up mountains, can be a strain on most car engines. Consult with a mechanic before making a decision. If this is the method selected, "tow bars" and "tow dollies" (for cars that will not fit on a "tow bar") can be rented from most truck rental agencies.

ADDITIONAL TRANSPORTATION COSTS

You may notice an extra charge for something which you never requested. A small charge may be listed under "additional transportation cost". These rates are approved by the I.C.C. and listed in each tariff book. They are based on the cost of doing business (cost of labor) in each county. It is sort of a "labor equalization factor". Rates can vary from zero to a few dollars for each 100 pounds.

There is a good reason for listing these rates separately. When loading or unloading a shipment, the driver often needs to request extra labor from a local agent. He may or may not have a partner who travels with him from one location to the next. Even if he does, he often needs a third or fourth person to help with loading or unloading.

The basic transportation rate does not incorporate all expenses incurred by the driver, in all circumstances. Therefore, the "additional transportation cost" is used to compensate the driver for the additional expense he may have when "doing business" in an expensive county.

STORAGE
(WHEN THE NEW HOME IS NOT READY)

If your new residence is not immediately available for occupancy, warehouse storage may be needed at origin or destination. The rate for each 100 pounds for storage-in-transit (S.I.T.) can vary between companies and counties. Since one county can be cheaper than another, ask each representative for the rates in your present location, as well as the destination county. There can be a huge price difference. (All costs related to S.I.T. are usually not discounted.)

The moving company is allowed to hold a shipment in S.I.T for up to 90 days. The rates are usually not guaranteed, but even if an increase should occur while your goods are in storage, it probably would not be excessive.

Individual rates per 100 pounds are calculated for: the first day in warehouse, each additional day (up to 90 days in total), warehouse handling, and pickup or delivery labor. In addition, a small charge will be assessed for valuation coverage for each month in storage (unless you specifically waive this).

After the S.I.T. period exceeds 90 days, the interstate nature of the shipment terminates. All costs will usually change since they become subject to the rates, terms, and conditions of the local warehouse. Charges for storage, as well as all labor costs, will no longer have to be based on poundage or I.C.C. regulations. The entire shipment will convert to "permanent storage" status and a separate contact with the local warehouse will be needed. When the conversion takes place, the prices will sometimes be more, sometimes stay the same, and often they will decrease. It will depend on the "cost of doing business" in that particular community.

Flatbed Truck – Wooden storage vaults are placed on a flat truck.

When trying to decide whether to have your possessions stored at origin or destination, another factor in addition to cost, needs to be considered. Individual circumstances determine what will be *most convenient*. If you are sure that you will need to remove items from the warehouse, you will want everything stored where you plan on being. Regardless of cost, you may have no choice. If removal of items is necessary, you can expect to pay an "access charge" for someone in the warehouse to help find what you need to remove. This is done on an hourly basis.

Removal of items can be a costly proposition. When your shipment arrives, it will probably be placed into large plywood containers. They are called "pallets" or "vaults". A forklift is used to move and stack these containers once they are sealed shut. Trying to figure out which container has the items you need to remove is like trying to find a "needle in a haystack". This is why the hourly "access charge" can add up.

If all of the related costs are similar at both origin and destination, and there are no extenuating circumstances, it is wise to have your shipment stored at destination. Once you are ready for final delivery, local arrangements can be made quickly and easily. A local phone call or visit to the nearby warehouse will certainly be more convenient.

If you are contemplating having your shipment delivered to a "public storage" facility, certain considerations need to be addressed. You will need to *carefully inspect everything for damage and/or loss* during the unloading process. Even though you are allowed 9 months after delivery to file a claim, if you make separate arrangements to move everything from a public storage facility, the company that delivered the shipment will undoubtedly fight a future claim. If you didn't make notations on the driver's inventory sheets at origin or at delivery, the company will probably take the position that the damage or loss occurred after it relinquished the shipment.

The biggest benefit in using a public storage facility is your ability to remove items at no extra cost. In addition, there is no warehouse labor cost to place everything into "pallets", and sometimes the monthly storage cost can be lower.

Since the movers will be taking their furniture pads with them, you will need plenty of blankets or padding. Ask the manager of the storage facility where they can be rented on a monthly basis. You will need to adequately protect all items being placed in the cubicle, and when loading a truck in the future. Do not be skimpy in this department.

Storage Vaults – A forklift is used to stack wooden vaults inside the warehouse.

SECTION 7

PACKING

"If I need to move one more time, all I will need is a little wagon."
  - Fred, a retired air force colonel who has "weeded out" his possessions 15 times in the past 20 years.

WHAT TO KEEP AND WHAT TO DUMP

A popular misconception is that it's cheaper to send a larger shipment. While it is correct to assume that the rate (amount of dollars for each 100 pounds) decreases as the size of a shipment significantly increases, you must keep in mind that the "multiplier" increases. So, before you start thinking about whether you or the moving company will perform the grueling task of packing, the entire family should engage in a "sort and weed" routine. The goal is to lighten the load as much as possible. Family members should objectively decide what they *really* will have a need or use for at destination. The borderline items should be part of a group discussion.

Everyone has sentimental or "maybe-some-day" STUFF. The daughter in high school has "Jake", the wooden

"This is easy, but what do I do with the goldfish?"

horse she rode while in kindergarten; the mother has 10 cast iron skillets, but only uses her favorite one for cooking each day; the father has two walnut antique dressers that he was supposed to refinish 15 years ago; the son has every pair of shoes and sneakers worn since grammar school and he is now in medical school; and the list of STUFF goes on and on!

Designate an area in the garage, basement or attic where everyone can slowly place the "dumpers". When the process is complete, plan a garage sale. When it is over, invite relatives, neighbors or friends to stop by and select what they need. In doing so, you will leave the community with a lot of happy faces bidding farewell. Lastly, call a charitable organization such as the Salvation Army or Goodwill Industries. They will usually send a truck to pick up the remaining items. However, sometimes you may be stuck bringing everything to them. In either case, make sure you get a receipt. You may be able to qualify for a charitable tax deduction on an itemized income tax return with the IRS.

Even though a few decisions will be made on a sentimental and personal basis, many can be logical and practical. Let's explore some typical considerations.

Alcoholic Beverages. They are illegal to include in an interstate shipment of household goods.

Appliances. Washers, dryers, stoves, dishwashers, refrigerators, and freezers are typically the most expensive items to move. Each one can sometimes cost $100-$200 to relocate. If any of these appliances are old or not performing like they used to, they are likely candidates to sell. Placing a "Classified" advertisement in the local newspaper may be the answer. If you are selling or renting your residence, maybe the purchaser or future tenant would be interested.

Even if an appliance is relatively new, you must decide whether or not you have a need for it in your new home. Many houses, apartments and condominiums contain built-in stoves, dishwashers and trash compacters. In addition, some homes are "all electric". A gas stove or dryer will not easily plug into an electrical outlet. It would be a shame to needlessly pay for moving these items. Also, the size and/or color of the appliance may not be appropriate with the new decor. In some cases, it is wise to use the money from selling an appliance, *plus the money saved by not moving it,* toward the purchase of a new one at the other end.

Books. (Read section called "Using the Post Office".)

Clothing. For clothing which is presently hanging in a closet, wardrobe cartons can be purchased. When full, these boxes can weigh 70-100 pounds. In addition to being heavy, the box alone costs about $8. Therefore, seriously consider dumping all clothing which is badly worn out or outdated. If there are suits with real wide lapels, try flapping them vigorously for a few minutes. If the lapels are big enough, maybe you can fly to your new home very economically!

Firewood/Lumber. They both are "no-no's" unless you have an abundance of money to transport these heavy items.

Flammables/Pressurized Containers/Combustibles/ Explosives, Etc. All categories are "no-no's". The inside of a truck can get extremely hot, since there are no windows for ventilation. All types of aerosol cans (even deodorants, hair sprays, shaving cream, etc.) have the potential to explode. All fuel in power tools, lawn mowers, etc. should be drained.

Propane in tanks should also be emptied. If you have a portable outdoor gas grill for cooking, light the grill a few days before moving (with the top open, of course). Allow the propane to totally burn itself out. If you try to release the propane gas without lighting the grill, the entire neighborhood will be aware of it.

Food. Try to consume most of the food items before the packing begins. Canned goods are heavy and costly to transport. Limit the amount of food, and consider putting spices and lighter things in plastic sandwich bags, instead of heavy jars.

Furniture. It is important to *assess what your needs will be at the new residence.* This takes time and a lot of common sense. For example, if you are moving from a four-bedroom home into a two-bedroom apartment, you will probably have less space for storage. You will have fewer closets, less space in the garage and/or attic, and no basement. Unless you want your new home to resemble a rummage sale, you had better sell the unneeded furniture. Also, if the room sizes are smaller, you might not have room for 3 sofas, 2 loveseats and 4 upholstered chairs.

When going through these deliberations, consider what you *really need,* as well as what you *realistically have room to accommodate.* Both considerations are equally important throughout the entire weeding-out process. A floorplan, along with room dimensions in the new home, will prove to be valuable. If possible, ask the present owner, tenant, or real estate agent to send a copy.

Magazines. If you have an abundance, thumb through the ones that can be eliminated. "Let your scissors do the walking!" Cut out the recipes, articles or pictures of interest. It is time well spent, since a few hundred magazines can be reduced to one small box. This can save some bucks!

Piano/Organ. Only if you cannot live without it, and there is adequate space for proper placement. Since they are heavy, they will be expensive to move. In addition, you should expect to pay a handling charge, and the cost to have it retuned at destination.

Plants. (Read section called "Transporting Plants".)

Pool Table. Only if you still use it; only if there is a room that it will comfortably fit into; only if it is worth the cost of transportation and special handling charges. If it has a slate surface, it should be completely disassembled. For safety, the slate should be placed in a wooden crate. At destination, someone will have to reassemble the pieces. It can be an expensive endeavor.

Record Albums. They are extremely heavy. A small box of records can be as heavy as tools or books (50 pounds or so). Weed out those which no longer appeal to your taste. The ones that are badly scratched and have a chorus of "stutterers" should be the first to go.

Telephone Book. Pack the telephone book from your present community. You will be surprised to discover how helpful it will be in the future. Most people discard it, then a year later, need to find an address or telephone number for some sort of communication. It can be especially useful during a holiday season when you need addresses for sending greeting cards.

Things attached to walls/ceilings. In general, items attached to walls or ceilings are usually better off staying there. They look attractive while attached, and can increase the total amount you are able to sell or rent the house for. Once removed, the area left behind can often resemble a wall or ceiling that was used for target practice with a shotgun. Also, before removing anything attached to the house, be sure you are legally permitted to do so. Items such as ceiling fans, built-in shelving, lighting fixtures, outdoor TV antennas, etc. are sometimes not included in the sale of a house.

Tools. Since they are extremely heavy, you will have to decide if you really need 5 hammers, 25 screwdrivers and 10 pairs of pliers. If you have accumulated an abundance of duplicate tools, try to eliminate the ones in the worst condition. It only takes one hammer to drive a nail into a piece of wood. Plus, when was the last time you broke a hammer?

If you are driving a car to the new location, place your toolbox in the trunk. That translates into 50 pounds of weight you are not paying to move, and it can be useful in an emergency. Lastly, since you will probably arrive at destination before the truck, the tools will be handy for odd jobs that need immediate attention.

Valuables. Do not include as part of the shipment. Make separate arrangements for their transportation. (Read the section explaining "liability protection" for further information on this subject.)

THE PROFESSIONAL PACK JOB

It's definitely a real treat to have experienced, professional packers perform the entire job. It is also interesting to watch. However, it can also be expensive. You will pay for each box provided, as well as a separate labor charge, based on the size of each container.

If you request the company to pack everything, it will usually send 1 or 2 packers on the day prior to the truck's arrival (unless a weekend or holiday is involved). They will pack everything, except items you need to use until the truck arrives. If requested, the packers will leave a few boxes behind which the driver can finish packing. Boxspring and mattress containers, a wardrobe box, and maybe a box in the kitchen are typical examples. (By the way, it is a good idea to plan on dining out the night before departure.)

The price for a professional pack job can be drastically reduced if you are willing to do some of the work. Non-breakable items such as books, tools, pots and pans, tupperware, silverware, linens, bedding and clothing are easy to do. Just packing these items yourself can drastically cut the packing cost.

You may request the company to only pack items of a fragile nature (china, crystal, glassware, lamp bases, pictures, mirrors, bric-a-brac, etc.). Not only is this convenient and safe, but it also helps to avoid a battle later on if a damage claim needs to be filed. If you did the packing, the "Was it packed properly?" question usually will surface with the moving company claims department. (Read the section on "liability coverage" for more details.)

THE DO-IT-YOURSELF PACK JOB

Packing is not a difficult chore. It requires some common sense, proper supplies, adequate planning, and a whole lot of time. It's a good idea to start packing a few boxes each day, at least one month prior to the move. Slowly whittle away at items that will not be needed during that time. You should be able to live without most items in the garage, attic, and basement. Many of the things contained in cupboards and closets can be placed in boxes a few weeks prior to moving. Designate an area in the garage, or in a spare room, for stacking the boxes.

During the last month, you will have prospective purchasers or tenants, neighbors, friends, and family members cruising through the house. Your goal is to have the residence appear as normal as possible. Pictures and wall decorations should remain hanging until a few days before the move.

Tell all family members that once they start packing a box, they should finish the job and place the box in the designated area. It can be very unsightly and embarrassing to have visitors walk by a room with assorted piles of "stuff" covering every inch of floor space. If you do not try to control the situation from the very beginning, your quaint home may look like General Sherman and his troops just rode through!

OBTAINING BOXES

There are a few ways to cut the cost of purchasing boxes, without sacrificing safety. However, you must start the "box shopping" routine a few months ahead of time. *This step can often reduce the total moving cost by $100-$200.*

The best place to obtain free, sturdy boxes is at the local liquor store. Since these boxes are designed to carry the weight of heavy liquor bottles, they are prefect for packing books, tools, silverware, and even your delicate glassware. (Many have cardboard dividers in them.)

You will need to "cut a deal" with an employee. Ask which day they receive most of their deliveries and stock the shelves. That is the best time to return. Since most stores have very limited storage space, they will usually cut the tops off of

"Remember, only the *empty* boxes are free!"

boxes, crush them, and throw them into a dumpster. Unless you receive a prior commitment, most stores will not have a nice variety to choose from. *Select only sturdy boxes with tops,* since all containers will need to be sealed shut and stacked.

Supermarkets also want to get boxes out of their way. As soon as the contents go on a shelf, the box is cut and thrown out. Prior arrangements should also be made at these stores. You can usually obtain some larger-sized boxes at a supermarket, but make sure they are sturdy. If they are not, do not use them. You do not want a truck full of accordians unloaded at destination. You will sometimes find fruit boxes with telescoping tops and bottoms. They are usually sturdy and can be used for larger-sized items.

A local record dealer is a good source for small boxes. Computer or office supply stores are also a great source. Cartons used to deliver heavy products are usually sturdy.

Friends, neighbors, and relatives are great sources. Many people collect boxes in their garage, attic or basement areas for use sometime in the future. After a few years, they accumulate an abundant supply for which they probably have no immediate or long range plans to use. Ask to partially "tap into their stash" since it can always be replenished.

Technically, it is illegal for a moving company to give "free-bees" to a customer, "as a condition for doing business" on an interstate move. It is considered an illegal "rebate". However, some companies pile discarded, used boxes outside of their warehouse. They acquire them from people who request unpacking. When an employer is paying for a relocation, this request is fairly common. When the driver goes to the local warehouse to return his paperwork, he usually has some used boxes to contribute to the pile. It may be beneficial to drive by a few moving companies to see if they have an assortment of discarded boxes. The trip could save you a lot of time and money if it is fruitful. "Nothing ventured, nothing gained!"

If you must purchase boxes from a moving company, you should expect to pay a hefty price for cardboard. It is most convenient, but also most expensive. You may want to limit these purchases to mattress and wardrobe boxes. They are very bulky, cumbersome, and difficult to transport with a car.

There are a few cheaper sources available if you must purchase them. Some of the larger truck rental agencies sell boxes and other types of packing supplies. Their prices are usually lower than those of the moving companies. Thumb through your local Yellow Pages under the "Moving-Truck Rental" section. Call a few agencies to get an idea of prices. If you need a large supply, they are sometimes cheaper "by the dozen".

Another source is available when a large supply of containers is needed. It is sometimes possible to purchase boxes directly from the companies that manufacture and distribute them. Look in the Yellow Pages under "Containers, Corrugated". Be sure to call before going to their place of business, since many do not sell directly to the public. Also, some may have a minimum amount that must be purchased.

SETTING UP SHOP (SUPPLIES NEEDED)

One secret to packing like the professionals is to have the proper materials and an organized environment. Without the proper "tools", the completed job will be mediocre at best.

Using the kitchen table as a work area is usually most convenient. When packing in rooms which are quite a distance from the kitchen, use a card table as your portable work station. Tape plastic to the surface of the table. It will prevent ink on the newspaper from rubbing off and soiling the surface.

Newspaper. If you do not mind having black hands at the end of the process, newspaper is still a cheap and effective packing material to use. It is the same type of paper used by the professionals, except the paper has ink on it. Since it does smudge, certain precautions need to be taken. As long as the newsprint does not directly touch the items being packed, damage from the ink should not occur. The trick is explained next!

Trash Bags/Baggies. Buy a healthy supply of large sandwich bags and various-sized trash bags. They can be used for all items that can be soiled by newspaper ink. Linens, clothing, small appliances, and lamp shades are typical examples. Dishes and glassware can be prewrapped in small plastic bags to eliminate the need to wash them when unpacked. These bags can also be used for packing food items, and for small amounts of nails, screws, nuts, bolts, etc.

Twist-Ties. Use the leftovers from a package of trash bags to secure all electrical cords on small appliances.

Bubble Wrapping/"Peanuts". If you buy special styrofoam products, use them only on the more valuable and delicate possessions. For most of your packing needs, newspaper is just fine.

Tissue Paper. Should be used instead of plastic bags for packing silverware and other silver items. Do not allow newspaper to directly touch silver.

Tape. The easiest to use is the 2"-3" wide plastic tape. It also provides the strength needed to adhere to a variety of surfaces. The tape that needs to be moistened with water is cumbersome to use, and will not hold as much weight. Masking tape is not as strong as the plastic variety, and tends to "get unglued" in a warm climate.

Razor Blade Knife. Can be used for cutting tape and also to cut cardboard when constructing an odd-shaped box. It's easier to use than a pair of scissors.

Felt-Tip Marker. Get a few different colors for writing the contents, as well as "special instructions" on the sides of each box ("This Side Up", "Fragile", etc.).

PROPER LABELING

Once a box is packed, use a felt-tip marker to indicate which room it will be placed in, and to itemize its contents. If

Labeling – List the contents on the *side* of each box. Also, be sure each container gets an inventory sticker.

the professionals do the packing, work along with them to be sure the contents of each box gets itemized on the *side of the container*. They will only make general notations such as "master bedroom-linens". You want to place your own list of contents on the side of each box, since some may need to be stored alongside a wall in the new basement, garage or attic area.

A common mistake is to make notations on the top of a box. Once they are stacked on top of each other, the notations are no longer visible. You are forced to shuffle them around in order to find the exact one desired. This can be time-consuming and rough on your back muscles.

On moving day, the movers will place inventory numbers on all boxes and other items to be loaded on the truck. These labels do not describe the contents or corresponding room locations where boxes should be placed at destination. To save yourself and the movers a lot of time, aggravation, and extra work, make sure each box is clearly labeled explaining room location and contents.

Avoid using the word "miscellaneous" to describe contents of a container. If you don't know how to describe your 25-year old collection of unneeded, unwanted, unused and ugly Christmas gifts, then simply use the description just mentioned. If "miscellaneous" is written on the box, you are sure to open it a few times each year while looking for something else. That kind of surprise, you don't need!

Several of the larger interstate moving companies provide free gummed labels that are contained in their informational booklets. They say "Fragile", "Do Not Load", etc. Ask each representative for a booklet explaining the company's services.

TYPICAL BOX SIZES

Small Box (1.5 cubic feet) - 13" X 13" X 16" - Commonly referred to as a "book carton". To give you an idea of its size, if you stand record albums on edge inside the box, they fit perfectly. It is ideal for small, heavy items (books, record albums, paper products, canned goods, small appliances, tools, etc.). If you pack any of these items in a large box, the bottom may fall out when lifted. Cardboard and tape are not strong enough to hold an excessive amount of weight. If you "over-pack" a box and the bottom falls out, it will be tough to blame the movers. Remember the old adage, "A word to the wise should be sufficient!"

Medium Box (3 cubic feet) - 18" X 18" X 16" - This size is twice the size of the small box (book carton). It should be used to pack most of what remains (except large items), after the heavy items are placed in the small boxes. Typical examples are pots, pans, kitchen items, shoes, purses, food stuffs, stereo components, garden supplies, toys, etc.

Even though there is a specially designed "dish-pak" container available for packing dishes and glassware, you may want to consider using medium or small boxes. If you are an inexperienced packer, it is easy to make the mistake of placing certain types of fragile items at the bottom of a "dish-pak" which cannot endure the excessive weight (70 pounds) on top of them.

Large box (4.5 cubic feet) - 18" X 18" X 24" - Should be used for light-weight, bulky items such as lamp shades, pillows, blankets, bedspreads, etc. Avoid placing fragile items in this size box since it is not as sturdy as a "dish-pak".

Disk-pak (6 cubic feet) - 18"X18"X30" - This is specially constructed to hold the weight of heavy, fragile items. The cardboard is twice the thickness of a normal box. It usually includes cardboard dividers to separate each item, and can be used for fragile items such as lamp bases, dishes, china and glassware.

Mirror/Picture Box - A telescoping carton that can be adjusted to protect glass, mirrors, pictures and paintings. (For extremely delicate or larger items, specially constructed wooden crates should be utilized.)

Wardrobe Box - 21" X 24" X 48" - A huge box with a metal bar (approximately 2 feet) extending across the top. Clothing presently hanging in closets can stay on the hangers. It eliminates the need to spend endless hours ironing clothes at destination. It can also eliminate a huge dry-cleaning bill for suits and dresses. If curtains, draperies or hanging plants need to be packed, this box is the answer.

It is also great for tall objects that will not fit into other containers. In addition, you will sometimes have unused space at the bottom which can be used for pillows, shoe boxes, or other lightweight items. That means a few less boxes you need to buy.

Mattress/Boxspring Carton - These boxes are individually designed to fit various bed sizes. They protect against soiling and snags. It is easy to rip the bottom of a boxspring that has a thin fabric stretched over the wooden frame.

If it happens to be raining at the time of loading or unloading, the moisture may cause a mattress/boxspring to acquire a musty odor that can linger for months. The box helps to prevent this from occurring.

There is another benefit to using these boxes. They allow the movers to pack the truck with less liklihood of damage occurring to other items. They reduce the possibility of movement inside the truck due to bumps and road vibrations.

INDIVIDUAL CONSIDERATIONS

The following is a list of common household items that require packing or special attention. Continue to refer back to this section throughout the entire process.

Aerosol Cans, Paints, Explosives, or Anything Flammable - All categories are illegal to transport on an interstate shipment, when using the professionals. If you pack them in a box and try to sneak them on the truck, you will probably be liable for any damage that may result. These are definite candidates to sell or give away before moving.

Air Conditioner - Before you decide to take it, be sure the new residence has proper electrical wiring to accommodate the unit. Also, check the owner's manual to find out if any special parts need to be secured (compressor, etc.). If you cannot find the manual, try calling a local appliance dealer for recommendations.

Appliances (small kitchen items such as a toaster, blender, iron, food processor, etc.) - Place in a small box. Pack in an upright position after prewrapping in a small plastic or paper bag. Do not allow newspaper to come in direct contact with the item. If bags are not available, prewrap in tissue paper, then use regular newspaper to finish the job. Secure all electrical cords with a "twist-tie".

It is most convenient to pack all small appliances into the same boxes. It makes unpacking much easier to organize. Kitchen towels can be used to fill open areas in these boxes.

Barbeque (Propane Gas) - Before disassembling, light the grill (with top up) a few days beforehand. Allow the propane to "burn itself out".

Clean extra thoroughly to get rid of grease build-up. Place detachable parts and briquets into plastic bags. Put bags into a small box along with garden tools, etc.

Beds (Also see "Mattress/Boxspring") - Even though the movers will usually disassemble and reassemble regular bedframes, you may want to take the rails off before they arrive. This allows you to label each rail so they are placed in the correct position at destination. The rails and the crosspieces should be tied together with rope or tape.

If you have bunkbeds or a waterbed that needs to be disassembled, do this on the morning of your move. Professional movers will not usually disassemble these beds, unless you are willing to pay an extra labor charge.

Bicycles/Tricycles - Clean thoroughly and wipe off grease deposits that usually accumulate near the chain. Since they are awkward to pack inside a truck, slightly loosen the handlebars so they can be turned.

Books - Place them flat, in small sturdy boxes. Always alternate the bindings (spine) of hard-covered books. This helps to prevent the glue in the bindings from cracking. Stuff newspaper into open spaces to avoid movement.

If you have a large collection of books, read sub-section entitled "Using the Post Office" for money-saving ideas.

Bottles/Glass Jars - (See "Food" section.)

Cedar Chest/Trunk/Footlocker - There is no need to empty the contents, unless it contains fragile or heavy items. Fill with linens, bedspreads, comforters, towels, sweaters, etc. If the contents are not going to be immediately unpacked at destination, place mothballs inside.

China Cabinet - All removable shelving needs to be taken out. Glass shelves must be boxed. Wooden ones can be bundled and stood on end in a wardrobe container. If the doors can be locked, they should be. The drawers and storage space below can be used to pack towels and small pillows.

Clocks - Remove the pendulum, if possible, from grandfather, grandmother, and mantle clocks. Place the pendulum and other removable hardware (weights) in a separate box. If you have an older mantle clock that is very heavy, pack tightly in a small box by itself.

Clothes Hamper - If you plan on taking it, fill it with linens, towels, shoe boxes, pillows, etc. Then tape it shut like a box, if you can do so without causing damage to the finish.

Clothing (Hanging) - Wardrobe cartons are a real blessing. Be sure to use them. Face the hangers in the same direction on the bar. It will make unpacking much easier.

For all clothing and fabric items which will not be used immediately upon arrival at destination (especially seasonal items), put mothballs in the containers. If you have limited closet space in the new home, these wardrobe boxes can be used for storage of seasonal clothing in an attic or garage.

Clothing (In Dressers) - Can be left in the drawers. However, do not overload them with heavy items. Excessive weight can cause damage to the drawers.

If a dresser is extremely heavy and needs to be maneuvered up or down stairs or in an elevator, drawers should then be emptied.

If the dresser is being placed in storage, put moth balls in each drawer. When being stored for a long period of time, it is wise to pack clothing in sealed boxes. In either case, remember that it is better to have clothing smell like moth balls, than look like swiss cheese!

Do not use tape or rope to prevent drawers or doors from opening. The tape can stick to the surface and harm the finish. Also, constant rubbing from rope can cause damage. The movers should place furniture pads (blankets) over each piece of furniture. Then, large "rubber bands" are used to hold the blankets in place. They resemble the inner-tube from a bicycle. This procedure should adequately secure the drawers and doors.

Clothing (Boxed) - Most clothing can be placed into medium-sized boxes. Avoid using newspaper, unless plastic bags are used first. Road vibrations over a long distance can magically transform a white shirt into a gray one!

Curtains/Draperies/Window Treatments - Usually they are left behind for the new occupants to enjoy. It is unlikely you will have the exact size window and same color scheme in the new residence. If you decide to move them, consider leaving the shades intact. The new occupants will appreciate not having to tape newspaper or sheets over the windows.

If curtains and drapes are transported, place them on a hanger and hang in a wardrobe carton. This can save a few hours of standing in front of an ironing board at destination.

Curtain Rods - They should be tied in a small bundle. Small pieces of hardware can be put into little plastic bags and taped to each rod. If possible, stand the bundle on end, inside a wardrobe carton. Place a tall piece of cardboard next to any clothing to avoid the possibility of a snag.

Desk - For drawers containing small objects and/or office supplies, pack the contents in a box since these items will be jostled around. Unless the desk is extremely heavy, other drawers can be left intact. Simply stuff towels or newspaper in the drawers to prevent movement.

Dishes/Glasses/China - When packing all items that are breakable in nature, remember to "paper everything to death". Start by putting a few inches of wadded-up paper along the bottom, before you even begin. Place the heaviest items, individually wrapped in paper, at the very bottom (platters, large bowls, etc.). Save the more delicate pieces to pack in the upper layers. If you have a few small items (heavy sugar bowls, salt and pepper shakers, etc.), use them to fill the open spaces. Of course, even these small articles will need to be wrapped in paper. Never pack unwrapped items inside each other.

If you are using a dish-pak, you should have four or more layers when you are done. If a smaller-sized box is used, at least two layers will probably result. Place wadded-up newspaper in between each layer to make it level and to provide cushioning.

After packing the bottom layer with large bowls and platters, the next layer should contain large dishes. After that, the next layer should be smaller plates and saucers. The top layer should be reserved for the more delicate items.

Dishes, plates and saucers should be individually wrapped, then packaged together in bundles. After placing four or five similar-sized items in a bundle, wrap a few sheets of paper around the bundle to hold it together. *Always pack dishes, plates and saucers standing on edge in a box. Do not lay them flat!* This may sound strange, but there is less chance of damage when they are packed in an upright position. If you pack them on top of each other, in a flat position, the ones at the bottom of the pile may be subjected to more weight than they can handle.

Cups and glasses should be placed upside down (on their rims), after being individually wrapped in paper. If they are similar in size, you can "nest" three or four glasses together to form a bundle. Always prewrap each one, using a few small pieces of paper. You never want to have "glass-on-glass".

Stemware and figurines should be packed in dish-paks and/or cartons retrieved from a liquor store. They usually have cardboard inserts (dividers) that can be used to separate stemware, goblets and glasses. After each piece is individually wrapped, it should be placed upside down in a cubicle. If any space is left at the top of a cubicle, stuff paper in the open area.

With delicate pieces of stemware, avoid placing too much pressure on the base. Put tissue paper inside the goblet and around the stem, before wrapping in newspaper.

Always mark in bold print, on the side of a box containing fragile items, "Fragile-Glass" and draw arrows showing which end should stay in an upright position. Also, state "This Side Up" on each side of the container. You do not want these boxes placed on the truck in any position other than the way they were packed.

Dressers (Also see "Clothing-In Dressers") - Remove attached mirrors, and place into mirror cartons/glass packs. If the casters come off easily, remove them. Place the screws and other hardware in a plastic bag. Then, tape the bag to the inside of a drawer.

Dryer (Clothes)- (Read section on "Washer (Clothes)", and also refer to "Extras" section for additional information.)

Fans/Portable Heaters - If they are small enough to fit in a box, place them in one. Since the original box is probably constructed of thin cardboard, consolidate these small boxes into one sturdy container.

Even if you are relocating to a warm climate, do not discard these items. They will be useful in the future.

Filing Cabinet - Dump the contents no longer needed. If the drawers contain a metal plate that can be moved forward, position it so that the paperwork cannot move. If the cabinet can be locked to prevent the drawers from opening, do so.

Fireplace Tools - Thoroughly wash, bundle and place in a box. If you pack them in a box containing other living room items, be sure to prewrap in a plastic bag. Consider placing in a box containing your odd-shaped garden tools, etc.

Food - Consume as much as possible before packing begins. Discard all perishables and the opened jars/cans. Remaining canned goods should be placed at the bottom of a small or medium-sized box. Dry goods can be placed at the top. Use newspaper between layers.

Glass jars/bottles should be individually wrapped in newspaper. Make sure all lids are tightly secured. Use tape to prevent opening due to road vibrations. It is a good idea to put liquid food containers into plastic sandwich bags, before placing in a box. Stuff newspaper into unfilled areas. You do not want maple syrup covering the contents, or leaking out of the box!

If your shipment is going to be stored for a long period of time, consider dumping all food items. Otherwise, you may have boxes full of moldy food or bugs greeting you in your new home.

Furniture (Small Articles) - The general rule-of-thumb is "if it will conveniently fit into a box, put it in one!" The movers want as much uniformity as possible, to fit everything tightly on the truck. They pack the inside of a truck like you would pack a box. Small, oddshaped items make it very difficult. Articles such as magazine/wine racks, stacking tables that disassemble, small plant stands, etc. should go into boxes.

Garden Hose/Tools - Thoroughly drain the hose, and screw one end into the other. Then, put into a medium-sized box or trash can with other small garden tools. Long-handled garden tools (rakes, shovels, brooms, etc.) should be tied or taped in bundles.

Lamp Base (Table) - Tall, narrow boxes can be purchased that are specially made for large table lamps. A dish-pak container can also be used, especially if there are several lamp bases that can be packed into one box.

Remove the lightbulb, shade and the "harp" that the shade rests on (if it removes easily). The electrical cord can be wrapped around the base.

Place a generous supply of wadded-up newspaper at the bottom of the box to act as a cushion. Wrap several sheets of paper around the entire base. Then, fold down excess paper at the top and bottom so that it is completely covered. Tape down the top, bottom, and all sides to hold paper in place.

When there are several bases being packed into one box, alternate the top of one with the bottom of another. This helps to get a tighter fit inside the box. Place wadded-up paper along the sides, and in any open areas of the box to prevent movement. Do not pack dishes or other heavy breakable items on top of the bases if they are laid in a flat position. As a matter of fact, if they can be placed in a vertical position, they are better off.

Use plenty of newspaper, just as you would when packing dishes, glassware or china. Don't be skimpy! Be sure to write "Fragile" and "This Side Up" on each side of the box.

Lamp Shades - Remove all shades, light bulbs, and metal shadeholders, if possible. Place shades in separate boxes, nesting smaller ones inside the larger ones. Do not use newspaper and do not pack other miscellaneous items into these boxes. The fabric can be easily dented, ripped, crushed, and soiled. Place each shade into a plastic bag, or use tissue paper to protect it.

When handling a lamp shade, always use the metal frame on top to avoid fingerprint marks. After packing other items, you are bound to have dirty hands. These stains will be very difficult to remove without harming the shade. Write "Fragile-Lamp Shades" on all sides of each box.

Lamp (Floor) - Remove shade and light bulb. The electrical cord can be wrapped around the base, or gathered together and tied with a twist-tie. Some floor lamps can be easily disassembled and placed in a box. Look for a metal nut under the base that can be removed.

Lawn Mower (Gas) - Gas and oil should be removed. Allow the motor to run until gas is gone. Leave the gas cap off for awhile. Drain the oil and detach the handle. Place the mower into a trash bag to prevent damage from leakage.

Linens (Towels, Sheets, Blankets) - Can be placed in drawers, as long as the furniture items do not become too heavy. Can also be used for packing. Use plastic bags or tissue paper to prevent soiling.

Liquor - Illegal to transport on an interstate shipment of household goods.

Mattress/Boxspring - Should be placed in special boxes that can be purchased from a moving company. Leave the slip covers on. They are easy to take off and put into a washer. Nobody has been ingenious enough to figure out a convenient method of placing a soiled mattress into a washer!

Microwave Oven - Pack it in the original box if you have it. If not, it can go the way it is. The movers will wrap a furniture pad around it.

Night Table - Remove all breakables. Stuff newspaper or towels into the top drawer so that the contents cannot move. If the bottom area has a door, place linen items inside. Since these tables are small, they will not get ridiculously heavy when packed.

Pictures (Small) - Should be individually wrapped, then placed side-by-side in the same box. Do not put one on top of the other. Use a sheet of tissue paper or plastic if the newsprint can smudge the picture. Stuff newspaper into open areas to prevent movement.

Pictures/Mirrors (Large) - Should be tightly packed into special boxes called "glass packs" or "mirror cartons". Use wide tape to criss-cross a large glass or mirrored surface. This helps to prevent breakage due to road vibrations.

Make-shift cardboard containers may be constructed from left-over cardboard boxes. If this is done, use plenty of paper to prevent movement, and to prevent the edges of the frame from being exposed. You do not want scratches on the frame, or the corners left on the front lawn!

Write "Glass-Fragile" on both sides of each container. Always place these boxes in an upright position, and never lay flat.

Special wooden crates should be used for extremely large pieces of glass or marble, valuable art work, delicate frames, etc. You can pay to have the moving company construct the crate, or do it yourself. Since getting a proper fit can be tricky for the do-it-yourselfer, find out what the cost would be to have it done professionally. It may be worth it.

For pictures, paintings, prints and frames of high value, describe separately and declare a value on all copies of the inventory. A photograph and an appraisal is highly recommended.

Pots/Pans - Place in medium-sized boxes using plenty of paper. Put a layer of wadded paper on the bottom. Individually wrap each item, then put more paper into any open spaces. Avoid a "shake, rattle, and roll" situation once the box is moved. Plus, do not pack any fragile items into these boxes.

Record Albums - Stand on end in small boxes. They fit perfectly inside the standard "book carton" that the movers use. Stuff paper into gaps to prevent movement. Albums that do not have covers should be individually wrapped in tissue paper to avoid scratches.

Refrigerator/Freezer - Unplug about 48 hours prior to loading.

Hopefully, you will have consumed or given away most of your food items by that time. Periodically, inspect the water tray under the appliance, and carefully empty as needed. You do not want a puddle of water to accumulate underneath. If it does, you can bet damage to the flooring will occur. Also, when the movers tilt the appliance to place it on a dolly, you do not want a trail of water dripping all the way out the door.

An automatic ice-making machine should be drained and properly disconnected from a refrigerator. Check the owner's manual for instructions, or consult with a professional appliance serviceman. Other precautions may also be necessary for your particular appliance.

Remove all shelving and trays, and pack separately in a box. Once the appliance is totally defrosted and drained, clean and dry thoroughly. Use paper towels to remove excess water. Leave the doors open, allowing all moisture to evaporate.

If you have small children, an emptied refrigerator/freezer can become a real hazard. Use rope to tie the door shut, after placing a block of wood inside to keep the door slightly open. In addition, advise your children to stay out of the room where the appliance is located.

Once the appliance is totally clean and dry, place baking soda inside to absorb musty odors. Coffee grounds or charcoal can also be used, but are messy to clean up. If you sprinkle baking soda on the bottom of each compartment, a damp sponge is all that is necessary at destination. If you insist on using coffee grounds or charcoal, use pantyhose or a nylon stocking for a container. Cut into sections, then tie a knot at both ends.

When the appliance is moved away from the wall, coil the electrical cord and tie with a twist-tie. Then, tape the cord to the rear of the appliance. Have cleaning supplies ready to wash the back end, as well as the floor area. It's amazing how much dirt and dust can accumulate through the years!

If you need to move any large appliance away from a wall before the movers arrive, here's a tip to make the job easier.

Spray a small amount of liquid glass cleaner on the linoleum floor at each corner that can be reached. This will help to "lubricate" the floor and make the job easier. Wipe up with paper towels when done. Since it is easy to damage linoleum when trying to "jocky" a heavy appliance out of a small area, you may want to wait until the movers do this.

Rugs - You should have rugs cleaned prior to moving day. It is a nice feeling to roll out spotless rugs in a new home.

All large rugs should be rolled up and tied. For added protection, a plastic dropcloth can be placed around the rugs before tying them.

Small rugs should be packed together in a large box. If storage is a possibility, use moth balls when rolling up or boxing any rugs.

Sewing Machine (Cabinet) - Remove the machine from the wood cabinet and place in a small box. Usually, it only requires removing a few screws. Place all hardware, bobbins, etc. into a plastic bag and pack into the same box.

Sewing Machine (Portable) - Can be placed in small or medium-sized box with other lightweight items. If it has a sturdy case, it is not essential to place in a box.

Shoe/Hat Boxes - Since these boxes are real flimsy, consolidate and place in sturdy boxes. If there is still unused space at the bottom of a wardrobe box, they can be placed there. However, do not overload this area. You do not want the bottom of the wardrobe to fall out.

Silver pieces - Do not allow newspaper or plastic to directly touch silver items. Tissue paper, special silvercloth, or a felt fabric is recommended. Use newspaper only for cushioning around each piece. If you have a silver chest containing tableware, stuff tissue paper inside to tightly secure the contents. Then, place at the bottom of a small box with other items.

If you have silver items of high value, consider packing them into a suitcase that will be traveling with you. If these items go on the truck, describe them separately on all copies of the inventory and declare a value for each item. Having pictures and an appraisal is a good idea. Purchasing the best "valuation coverage" available is highly recommended (full value replacement protection).

Stereo and Components - If you have the original boxes and packing materials, use them. Then, consolidate in a small or medium-sized box. Pack speakers to prevent a rip or puncture.

Most turntables have adjustment screws that should be tightened. Many will also have a small locking device to secure the arm (the part that contains the needle). Even if the arm does have a plastic lock, use tape to hold the lock in place. Also, tape down the record holder arm and anything else that can move, including the case. This will prevent movement of these delicate parts within the box.

If there are many little wires to unplug from different components, wrap masking tape around each wire and matching hole. Use a code that will make it easy for you to reassemble at destination. Otherwise, you may have to spend a day reading the owner's manual. Use plenty of newspaper to tightly pack each component in the box. Write on all sides of the box, "Fragile-This Side Up", indicating with an arrow which side is the top.

Stove - Thoroughly clean to remove grease build-up. Place removable parts in a box (trays, grates, knobs, etc.). If the burner elements do not easily remove, use tape to secure them.

Gas connections need to be disconnected from the outlet before the movers arrive. If you are unable to do the disconnecting, ask the moving company representative for the name of an appliance specialist whom you can call to provide this service. This should be arranged long before moving day.

Suitcase - Can be used as a packing container for non-breakable items such as sheets, towels, sweaters, etc. That translates into a few less boxes you will need to purchase.

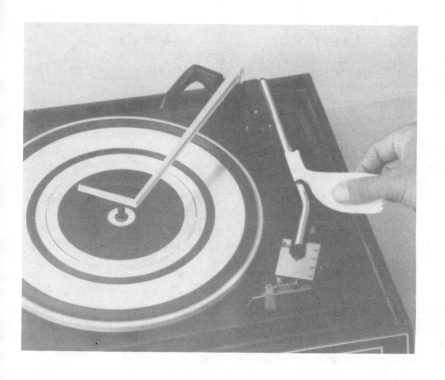

Turntable – Use tape to secure the arm and other moveable parts.

Television (Portable) - If the original box is still available, use it. If not, pack tightly in a box by itself to prevent damaging the screen or control knobs. While most movers will load a portable television by wrapping a furniture pad around it, a box provides better protection.

Always keep the television in an upright position. Never lay flat or on its side. Mark on the sides of the box "Fragile-This Side Up", so the movers know how to handle it. Expect to make a few minor adjustments at destination.

Television (Console) - Remove plastic knobs and place in a small plastic bag. A furniture pad will be wrapped around the entire unit.

Tools - If you have metal or wooden tool chests that can be tightly closed, use them. If not, pack all tools, nails, nuts, bolts, screws, etc. into small boxes. Plastic bags can be used to separate various sizes.

Cabinets, work benches, and dressers in the garage that are full of heavy items should be emptied. As you are doing so, properly label the outside of the box to make unpacking a breeze.

Tool Chest - If you are driving to the new residence, pack a small tool chest in the trunk. It may be useful on the trip in the event you experience mechanical problems. Most importantly, it will be useful at both ends for little chores that will need to be performed.

Toys - Large plastic toys can be placed in a large box. A clean trash can may be used if it can be tightly taped shut. If you are real industrious, you can individually wrap each item. However, if they are still in one piece, there is not too much the movers can do to these items to damage them!

Vacuum Cleaner - Clean the bag and transport in the trunk of your car, if possible. It is nice to have it available for use before the van arrives. It it does get loaded on the truck, ask the movers to load it last. In doing so, you are certain to have it unloaded before the furniture.

Valuables - Do not include in the shipment. Make separate arrangements to transport coin/stamp collections, valuable documents, jewelry, etc. If you are driving, never leave valuables behind in your automobile or motel room. Keep by your side at all times. There may be other people interested in traveling with your possessions!

Washer (Clothes) - (Also see "Extras" section for additional information) - Disconnect both hoses from faucet. Drain the hoses and allow them to thoroughly dry. If the appliance has a "spring-mounted" motor, it should be secured by "blocking" it. Hoses and the electrical cord should be taped to the back. Check the owner's manual or call an appliance dealer for more specific instructions about your machine.

If this all sounds too complicated, call a serviceman to perform this task. If you are willing to pay the transportation cost, do not be skimpy when thinking about the additional cost to have any appliance properly prepared for the trip. When all is said and done, you want an appliance to work properly when it arrives at destination.

A styrofoam "washer block" can be purchased from the moving company to prevent the tub from rotating. Towels or folded pieces of cardboard can be tightly wedged into the space between the top of the tub and side walls to provide bracing. This will prevent the tub from bouncing around every time the truck hits a bump in the road.

If you are moving during the winter months, do not use any appliance that circulates hot water until it reaches normal room temperature (wait a few days). When the appliance is cold, real hot water can cause damage. This also applies to dishwashers.

PACKING A "CAR-BOX"

If you are traveling in an automobile, handy items can be placed in a small box on the back seat or floor. Here are some suggestions.

- Aerosol tire inflator
- Camera
- Emergency tools
  (if tool box is not going)
- Flashlight
- Games/toys for children
- Litter bag
- Napkins
- Road Maps
- Snacks
- Sunglasses

Of course, do not forget items that should go in a wallet such as a driver's license, credit cards, car ownership/ registration card and insurance card.

PACKING THE
"KEEP WITH YOU AT ALL TIMES" SUITCASE

Since valuables should not be included in a shipment of household goods, they always present a transportation problem. If these items are going to accompany you in the car, they can be packed in a suitcase or a box. In either case, do not leave the container unattended. The following is a partial list of what you may need to make special arrangements to transport:

- Bank account books
- Coin/stamp collection
- Currency of any kind
- Insurance policies
- Jewelry
- Medical/dental records
- Precious metals or stones
- School records for children
- Valuable documents

PACKING A "QUICK-FIX BOX"

There are certain things you may need immediately upon arrival at destination. These items should be placed in a box and taken in the car. If you are flying, inquire about checking the box in along with your luggage. For that matter, a suitcase could be used instead of a box! Since you will arrive at the new home before the movers, it will be helpful to have some basic essentials. The trick is to minimize what you have to buy. Limit your purchases to those items which are impractical or dangerous to take. The following is a list of the most common items to pack in your "Quick-Fix Box":

134

- Alarm clock
- Cleaning supplies (rags, plastic bucket, paper towels, cleanser, glass cleaner, plastic trash bags, disinfectants (non-aerosol)
- Coffee pot (coffee filters, powdered milk, sugar)
- Cooking utensils (paper plates and cups, napkins, plastic glasses and silverware, frying pan, cooking pot, bottle opener, can opener)
- Extension cords
- First aid box (aspirin, band aids)
- Flashlight and candles (take a few, since the electricity may not be turned on)
- Foods (coffee, tea, cereal, salt and pepper)
- Fuses
- Games (a few small items to keep the children out of your hair)
- Light bulbs (an assortment of various sizes)
- Radio with batteries
- Sheets (to cover windows)
- Shelving paper and thumb tacks
- Tape measure
- Toiletries (soap, toilet paper, facial tissues, towels, shampoo)
- Tools (hammer, screwdriver, pliers, wrench, scissors, three-way electrical plug, small assortment of various-sized nails and screws)

NOTES:

SECTION 8

USING THE POST OFFICE
AND OTHER ALTERNATIVES

"Active participation does pay off ."
- Jim and Mary, after saving big bucks by taking their
library of law books to the Post Office.

If you are interested in saving money and willing to accept a small amount of inconvenience, a variety of alternatives are available for shipping a portion of your household goods.

Big savings can be derived by sending some of your boxes through either the Post Office; privately owned "parcel carriers"; interstate bus companies; the railroad; or the airlines. Even though they charge according to the weight of a box and the miles traveled (except the airlines), their rates are usually less than an interstate moving company.

Use the telephone book to find out the current rates, packing requirements, or other conditions they may have. You will discover a big variance. Find out what kind of insurance is included in their normal rate structure, and the cost for additional coverage you may need. Also, even though you may not be able to include boxes of "breakables" when using a few of these methods, those boxes can be placed on the moving van. As a matter of fact, you should plan on including all boxes containing breakable and fragile items with your shipment of furniture going with the moving company. Remember, the less handling, the less chance of breakage!

Most interstate moving companies have a 1000 pound minimum. In addition, the rate for each 100 pounds is extremely high for these shipments. Therefore, if you only need to transport a few furniture pieces and a dozen boxes, you should definitely consider selling the furniture and utilizing an alternate method for shipping the boxes. If you insist on using a moving company, you can expect to "pay the piper".

A few telephone calls and a little "leg-work" can often save hundreds of dollars. You must decide whether any of these methods are appropriate for your situation.

THE POST OFFICE

While the Post Office will ship boxes containing small household items and personal effects, *the biggest bargain can be achieved when books need to be moved.* The government actually gives you a break in this department! When you inquire about rates for shipping books, make sure you ask for the "Special Fourth Class Book Rate".

Using this method can sometimes save more than 50% of the cost of moving books with a moving company. If you have more than a few boxes, it's definitely worth a trip to the local P.O.

Before preparing books for mailing, check with your local P.O. for the current postage rate. You will be pleasantly surprised to discover that the cost is the same, no matter how many miles the books must travel within the United States.

Once you determine the cost for two 50 pound boxes of books ($17.28 in 1987), compare that price with the "rate per

100 pounds" that the moving company will be charging to transport books on its truck. Compute the difference in price for every 2 "book cartons" you deliver to the P.O. Then, multiply that amount times every 2 "book cartons" to be shipped. You will soon discover how a little effort on your part can save money.

P.O. Cost For Shipping Books Anywhere Within The U.S. (1987 Rates):

Per Container: 69¢ for the first pound
25¢ for each additional pound (up to 7)
15¢ for each pound (after 7 pounds)
(70 pounds maximum)

Example : 50 pounds of books (one small box) = $8.64
100 pounds of books
(two small boxes) = $17.28
1000 pounds of books
(twenty small boxes) = $172. 80

P.O. Weight Limitations On Any Box:

Each box is limited to a maximum of 70 pounds. When shipping books, it is doubtful that a box much larger than a "book carton" would be allowed. (When fully packed, it can easily weigh 70 pounds.) In addition, since you have to bring them to the P.O., you do not want them much heavier than 50 pounds.

Use a bathroom scale to be certain you stay within the weight limitation. Don't get stuck repacking boxes at the P.O.

P.O. Size Limitations On Any Box:

They will not accept any box that has a sum total of more than 108 inches. This is calculated by adding the length to what is called the "girth".

U.S. POST OFFICE

"What a great way to ship the library!"

Example: A standard size "book carton" used by a moving company is approximately:

> 17 inches long
> 13 inches deep (times 2)
> <u>13</u> inches tall (times 2)
> 69 inches in total

Be sure to label each box, identifying the contents as "BOOKS". Also, keep all shipping receipts. If you qualify to deduct moving expenses on your federal tax return, shipping expenses should be included as a deduction. (See separate sections in IRS rules.)

If you have a friend or relative willing to accept boxes at destination, consider shipping them one or two weeks in advance (books take longer to deliver). If you want to personally receive all boxes, drop them off on the day before departure. This should allow enough time for you to travel to destination. Of course, this is assuming you do not take a side trip.

OTHER PARCEL CARRIERS

Throughout the country, independent parcel-shipping companies are available to transport boxes. One of the most recognized names is United Parcel Service. Since there are others performing the same service, it pays to compare prices. They all have weight and size limitations that are similar to the P.O. Like the P.O., they have restrictions on the type of items allowed, as well as packaging requirements. Use the telephone to inquire about prices, restrictions and packaging information.

In most cities, you can also find "mail centers" that provide various kinds of shipping services. Many are franchise operations which utilize the services of many parcel carriers. While they are usually more conveniently located than the main office of an independent parcel carrier, they all charge a "handling fee" for each box they process (approx. $1.50-$2.00 per box). If you have numerous boxes, driving to the carrier's main office can save a few dollars on each box. However, if you must rent a truck or drive a substantial distance, it may not be worth the trip.

Most independent parcel carriers can usually deliver boxes within one to five days, depending on distance traveled. Therefore, you may want to have someone else receive them at destination if you are planning a leisurely drive by automobile.

U.P.S. provides free "valuation coverage" up to $100 per box. Additional coverage can be purchased at a cost of 25¢ for each additional $100 of declared value. Be sure to ask each company about its coverage. If something is worth the cost of shipping, it is worth protecting against loss or damage.

BUS COMPANIES

This alternative is also worth investigating, especially if you need to transport boxes weighing more than 70 pounds and/or larger than 108 total inches. One of the larger interstate companies which will transport boxes is Greyhound. Of course, you will have to make arrangements to pick up the shipment at a terminal. It does not provide door-to-door service.

Again, use the telephone to inquire about prices, rules and regulations. While each company is slightly different, they all base their prices on weight, distance and size of the boxes. One company may ship boxes which are up to 100 pounds and 141 total inches, and another may transport 150 pound boxes which are even larger. Some will transport boxes containing furniture and "breakable" items, and some will not.

With some companies, the price for each box will go down as the total number of boxes increases. For example, from one to ten boxes may be a certain amount, but ten or more may be cheaper for each box. Be sure to ask questions!

USING THE RAILROAD

Interstate railroad companies are another alternative for transporting boxes. Like the bus companies, they will ship "station-to-station". You will need to make arrangements for pickup at their facility. Having a friend available who has a pick-up truck or small van is always helpful.

Amtrak Economy Rail Express is one of the larger companies which is capable of shipping boxes from one end of the country to the other. Even though it will ship a box up to 4 feet long and 4 feet in width, it must not weigh more than 100 pounds. In addition, it has a 1000 pound maximum for each shipment. Since it has restrictions on what is allowed in boxes (no "breakable" or fragile pieces, furniture or appliances, etc.), call to get details before going to the terminal.

Like the moving companies, railroads also charge according to the weight and distance traveled. However, the good news is that their rates for each 100 pounds can often be one-half the price. Shipping 1000 pounds of boxed items across the country can translate into hundreds of dollars in savings.

AIRLINES

Each airline has its own set of regulations pertaining to the number of "pieces" allowed, as well as size and weight limitations. If you plan on flying, a telephone call to the airline office can often save money. Ask how many "pieces" each member of the family (even children) is entitled to check-in as baggage.

Let's assume that four tickets are purchased and each ticket entitles a person to 2 "pieces" of baggage. If you only have four suitcases, then four boxes may be entitled to a "free ride". If each box weighs 50 pounds, that means 200 pounds are not being loaded on the moving van. If you are paying a transportation rate of $50 for each 100 pounds, you just saved $100 by checking in four boxes at the baggage counter.

Once you determine how many "freebees" you may be entitled to, ask what the additional cost will be for each box that exceeds the limit. Let the airline know your intentions, and find out what procedures to follow at check-in time.

Some airlines offer a very inexpensive method for transporting boxes. However, the major problem is that you are forced to deal with the "hustle and bustle" at airports. You can usually obtain "curb service" by rewarding a porter with a reasonable tip! However, you will need a reliable person with a small van or pick-up truck to offer assistance at both ends of the trip. A taxi cab will not work.

If these details can be easily arranged, find out when you should have everything checked in. Normally, it is an hour or two prior to departure. If you are not driving to the airport in the same vehicle as your luggage and boxes, have the other vehicle follow you. You want to arrive at the "curb" at the same time. Allow enough time to avoid last-minute anxiety and nervousness, especially if you are traveling with children!

SECTION 9

"CASH REBATE" PROGRAMS,

AND OTHER HELPFUL SERVICES

"Moving companies have become extremely generous."
- The author

In this ever-changing deregulated industry, new programs and services are constantly being introduced. In addition, some may be changed, modified, or eliminated by the time your move actually takes place. Due to extreme competition, many companies are getting creative. A "trial and error" approach has produced some winners, as well as a few losers. *It is important to ask each company for details that will confirm all of the information provided. Also, inquire about new programs, services and conditions that may be in effect by the time your move takes place.*

Receiving a "Cash Rebate" When Selling and/or Buying a Home (From Allied Van Lines and Mayflower)

One of the most creative and innovative programs to develop as a result of deregulation, is presently offered by Mayflower and Allied Van Lines. If you plan on selling your home with the help of a real estate broker and/or purchasing a new residence through a real estate company at destination, these programs are worth consideration. *They can save hundreds, and potentially thousands of dollars in relocation expenses.*

If you are going to consider this type of program (which is free, by the way), you must start making arrangements much earlier in the relocation process. To receive the largest "cash rebate", you should make arrangements for a Mayflower and/or Allied representative to provide a cost estimate for your move, *prior to putting your house on the market and/or buying a new home at destination.*

This type of program reverses the traditional relocation process. It requires you to call the moving company first, instead of last. If you "can accept change", you may also be entitled to "accept a check" when the move has been completed!

Mayflower calls its program "C.A.R.E.S." (Allied's name for a similar program is "M.O.R.E.") The "cash rebate" from each program is additional bonus money that can go directly to you or the company which is paying for the relocation. Either moving company will make arrangements to have a check sent to whomever is predesignated to receive it. If a company is paying, and is aware you are enrolled in this type of program, it may want some or all of the "rebate" to help reduce its expenditure for the relocation. This must be prearranged between you, your employer (if applicable), and the moving company.

Each program is offered by the moving company through a national independent "real estate referral service". In order to benefit from the program, you must list your present home for sale and/or buy a residence at destination, through a real estate company which is approved by the referral service.

If you would like to use a particular real estate broker which is not already approved by the referral service company, make the company aware of this. Sometimes, it is able to obtain the cooperation of real estate brokers not presently enrolled in its program, but who are willing to accept its terms and conditions.

If you have not yet employed a real estate company to sell your house and/or purchase a new home at destination, these programs offer a tremendous money-saving opportunity. Here's how they work- Once you decide to move with either Mayflower or Allied, the representative for either company can enroll you in its program. Mayflower will enter you in its "C.A.R.E.S." program. Allied will enroll you in its "M.O.R.E." program. Each representative should be able to compute the maximum potential rebate to which you may be entitled. They will collect some preliminary facts and information about your present home, as well as basic information concerning your needs at destination. This information gets sent to the independently owned "real estate referral" company. It will work with you to find an acceptable real estate broker to sell your present home and/or find a new home to purchase at destination.

When you sell and/or buy a home through the mutually agreed upon real estate broker(s), and move with the company that enrolls you in its particular program, you are entitled to receive the rebate. *With Allied Van Lines, you can earn as much as $100 for every $10,000 of the sale price of either, or in some cases, both residences.* Mayflower's program offers a maximum of $50 for every $10,000 of the sales price, one half the rebate amount offered by Allied.

For example, let's assume you need to sell your present residence, and have not yet contracted with a real estate company. You list it with a real estate broker that is acceptable to the referral service working with Allied Van Lines. If your home sold for $100,000 it could entitle you to as much as a $1,000 cash rebate. The same principle applies to the purchase of a new home at destination. If you purchase a home through an approved real estate company for $100,000, you can potentially earn another $1000. (You would only be entitled to 50% of either rebate amount, if more than one real estate company is involved in the sales transaction or if developer/contractor discounts are involved.) Of course, you must move with the company that enrolled you in its program.

In the real estate industry, when two brokers are splitting a commission, it is called a "co-op" sale. One company puts the house on the market, but a different company finds a buyer and is entitled to a part of the commission for its efforts. Since a substantial percentage of real estate transactions are "co-op" sales, there is a good chance you may only be entitled to 50% of the "cash rebate". However, even if the sale or purchase becomes a "shared transaction", "half a loaf is better than no loaf at all!"

OBTAINING FREE "MOVING GUIDES"

Many interstate moving companies provide free brochures that not only contain helpful information, but also contain change-of-address cards and an ample supply of stickers to be placed on boxes and furniture. ("Fragile", "Do Not Load", etc.) If you need additional stickers, ask the company representatives for more. You should not have to purchase them!

"THE MOVING PICTURE"
FROM BEKINS VAN LINES

Bekins has taken the "moving guide" one step further. It has developed a 15 minute video-cassette which offers helpful advice concerning the relocation process. The same information is also available in a brochure, if you do not have a VCR machine for viewing. Contact your local Bekins agent if you want to make arrangements to receive either format. This free information is provided without obligation to use their services.

MAYFLOWER'S "MY MOVE"
MOVING KIT FOR CHILDREN

A colorful 24-page booklet is available from Mayflower, which was designed especially for children. A psychologist assisted in planning this material. As traumatic as uprooting a family may be for adults, children can also experience psychological difficulties. This booklet helps children deal with those problems. It contains colorful cartoons, stickers, games and other fun-filled activities. Ask its representative for a free copy when receiving your cost estimate.

ADDITIONAL FREE INFORMATION

The American Movers Conference provides three free pamphlets as a public service. "Moving and Children", "Guide to a Satisfying Move", and "Moving Pets and Plants". One or all three can be obtained by sending a stamped, self-addressed envelope to its office at 2200 Mill Road, Arlington, VA 22314.

OBTAINING INFORMATION
ABOUT YOUR NEW LOCATION

If you are moving to an unfamiliar area, it is a good idea to educate yourself beforehand. Try to get as much information as possible from friends, realtors and others who may be familiar with your new environment. A letter to the Chamber of Commerce or tourist bureau in the area can often be helpful.

Some of the moving companies provide free information about major cities throughout the country. Be sure to ask each representative about this!

Many of the larger real estate companies have an in-house relocation department that provides free literature. They are often affiliated with a separate relocation company. Read through the real estate section in your Sunday newspaper. You should be able to find a few advertisements which say something like - "Relocating? Call our office for free literature about your destination city!" The advertisement will either have a local telephone number to call, or a toll-free number. As long as it is free, helpful information, why not educate yourself?

UNITED'S "BETTE MALONE™ CONSUMER SERVICE CENTER"

In addition to providing detailed information on most U.S. cities, this free service provides 10 separate booklets explaining the ins-and-outs of an interstate move. It is one of the most comprehensive informational packages available from any moving company.

When receiving a cost estimate, its representative will probably give you United's Preplanned Moving Guide. This brochure contains a prepaid postcard that can be completed and mailed to the company. Within a few weeks, a large envelope should arrive that will provide you with a "library of literature".

BEKINS' "CONNECTIONS"™ MEMBERSHIP ($50)

Bekins Van Lines is affiliated with "Connections"™ Relocation Company. For a one-year membership fee of $50, they will enroll you in this program. It offers a wide variety of relocation assistance, as well as special discounts on services throughout the country.

BEKINS' "FIRST DAY SERVICE"

Bekins' movers will unpack boxspring containers and a few other miscellaneous boxes for free, providing the company did the packing.

BEKINS' "GUARANTEED SATISFACTION" PROGRAM

This program deals strictly with the performance of the workers while the actual labor is being performed (packing, unpacking, loading, and unloading).

If you are dissatisfied with the quality of work being performed, you are expected to inform those performing the labor. You must give them an opportunity to correct the problem. *If the quality of service continues to be dissatisfactory the company will refund the cost for that portion of the move.*

ALLIED'S "COMING HOME"™ SERVICE

Allied Van Lines guarantees a personal visit to your new residence by a representative of its company at destination, within 7 working days after delivery. If the residence is more than 50 miles from its closest agent, Allied guarantees you will at least receive a telephone call within 10 working days after delivery.

If Allied fails to comply with the terms and conditions of its guarantee, you will be reimbursed $50. All you need to do is fill in a small information card within 30 days after delivery, and forward it to the company.

This service is available on non-military interstate household goods shipments that weigh at least 3500 pounds. (They exclude shipments moving to or from Alaska and Hawaii.)

Allied offers this "personal touch" to display its commitment to the quality of service it provides. If any problems do develop, Allied assures you they will be given prompt attention.

THE "CREDIT PLAN" FROM
NORTH AMERICAN VAN LINES

Once you receive its credit approval, participating agents will provide financing arrangements for your interstate move. It is called the North American Payment Plan (NAPP) and is available on an individually-paid household goods relocation.

When your credit application is approved, you no longer have to worry about paying the driver at the time of delivery. It allows you to make payments in monthly installments. (As with most credit plans, you should expect to pay extra financing fees.) If this installment plan sounds interesting, ask its representative for more details.

THE INCREDIBLE "MONEY BACK GUARANTEE" FROM NORTH AMERICAN VAN LINES

(I've saved the best for last to make sure you are reading thoroughly.)

It may sound too good to be true, but it isn't! The company will promise to pick up and deliver a shipment within the agreed upon schedule, or *it will refund 100% of the transportation charge* (commonly called "linehaul charge").

No other company has been as confident in its system to put that much money where its mouth is. While others offer $100-$125 per day for each day they are late, North American has gone one step further.

If you are paying for the move yourself, and have over 4500 pounds of household goods (that is usually 4 rooms), ask its representative about this program. Some agents for the company (but not all of them) are allowed to place a few shipments each month on this program. Ask its representative if you qualify and about special conditions that may apply.

SECTION 10

TAX TIPS

"It is always a pain in the neck, but at least the federal government helps me get the kinks out ".
*   - Nick, a corporate executive who has relocated his family five times in the past twelve years.*

If you meet conditions established by the Internal Revenue Service, the federal government may soon become your best friend. However, when dealing with the IRS, you must always keep careful records of everything. Keep written receipts of all moving-related expenses before, during, and after the relocation.

Your tax advisor, or the local IRS office, will help to advise and decipher the deductions to which you may be entitled. There are many exceptions and "special circumstances" that can be applicable. Also, tax laws are frequently revised and changed. For instance, the IRS instituted a major change in the deductible moving expense category when it passed the Tax Act of 1986. It affects everyone who applies for moving expense deductions for 1987 onward. *Now, a taxpayer must file an itemized return to take these deductions.* Prior to 1987, you were allowed to deduct these expenses even if you filed a "short form". While this change may be of little significance to people who are homeowners since they would probably file an itemized return anyway, *it can have a dramatic impact on renters who are moving. If they file a "short form", they cannot take a moving expense deduction.*

Since the author is not an accountant, attorney, or expert on tax law, only general information and/or excerpts directly taken from IRS publications are provided in this section (IRS Publication #521 and Form #3903 provide complete explanations). Both can be obtained from your local IRS office. Also, your local Post Office or Public Library may stock these publications.

Here are some of the categories which are included in IRS Form #3903. Remember, there are many exceptions and special situations that may apply to you.

"Who may deduct moving expenses? - If you moved your residence *because of a change in location of your* job, you may be able to deduct your moving expenses. You may qualify for a deduction whether you are self-employed or an employee. However, you must meet certain tests of distance and time.

"Distance Test - Your new workplace must be at least 35 miles farther from your old residence than the location of your previous workplace. For example, if your old workplace was 3 miles from your old residence, your new workplace must be at least 38 miles from that residence. If you did not have an old workplace, your new workplace must be at least 35 miles from your old residence.

"Time Test - If you are an employee, you must work full time for at least 39 weeks during the 12 months right after you move. If you are self-employed, you must work full time for at least 39 weeks during the first 12 months and a total of at least 78 weeks during the 24 months right after you move.

"Moving Expenses in General - You may deduct most, but not all, of the reasonable expenses you incur in moving your family and dependent household members. You may not include moving expenses for employees such as a servant, governess, or nurse."

Examples of expenses you MAY deduct are:

• Travel - 80% of meal expenses, and lodging expenses during the move to the new residence.
• Temporary living expenses in the new location
• Pre-move travel expenses

Examples of expenses you MAY NOT deduct are:

• Loss on the sale of your residence
• Mortgage penalties
• Cost of refitting carpets and draperies
• Losses on quitting club memberships

Types of deductions allowed for moving your household goods and personal effects include: cost of packing, moving, crating, storage-in-transit, and insuring your possessions (liability coverage). Also, the cost of transporting your car to the new location. There is no dollar limit to these types of deductions!

There are other types of moving expense deductions that can be taken, but these categories have limitations on the total dollar amount allowed. All of these other expenses may not total more than $3,000. In addition, "househunting trip expenses" and "temporary living expenses" together may not be more than $1,500. These are overall per-move limits.

You may include most of the costs to sell or buy a residence or to settle or get a lease. Examples of expenses you MAY include are:

• Sales commissions
• Advertising costs
• Attorney fees

- Title and escrow fees
- State transfer taxes
- Cost to settle an unexpired lease or to get a new lease

Examples of expenses you MAY NOT include are:

- Costs to improve your residence to help it sell
- Charges for payment or prepayment of interest
- Payments or prepayments of rent

Reimbursements - You must include any reimbursements of, or payment for, moving expenses in gross income as compensation for services. If your employer paid for any part of your move, you must report that amount as income on Form 1040.

Even though you may have other expenses during the relocation process, don't expect to include everyone of them on the "Moving Expense" form. You may be entitled to a deduction in a different category of your tax return. Keep all of your receipts and consult with a competent tax advisor for more complete information. Only the very basic facts have been outlined in this section.

"They won't believe I actually have *good* news!"

SECTION 11

COUNTDOWN TO MOVING DAY

"First I was overwhelmed, then depressed, then angry, then organized."
　　- Connie, a disgruntled housewife who had all of the planning "placed on her lap" after her husband already started his new job 2000 miles away.

The following information will help to minimize last minute headaches and upset stomachs. Many people find themselves running around like a "chicken with its head cut off". While anxiety and nervousness are unavoidable, their levels can be greatly reduced. An organized plan which includes a timetable is extremely important. *It is the only way to reduce most of the last-minute chaos.*

Since all of the details outlined will not apply to your set of circumstances, check off the information that does. If necessary, make additional notations in the margin area. (A yellow felt-tip marker can also be used.) As you accomplish each task, cross it out. Constantly refer back to this timetable throughout the entire process.

157

SIX TO EIGHT WEEKS BEFORE:

- Start the "weeding out" process. Have each family member start eliminating unneeded, unwanted, and unused items.

- Sell or give away flammable items.

- Conduct a garage sale.

- Decide what you want professionally packed into boxes.

- Obtain estimates from at least 3 moving companies. Review all details and keep asking questions.

- Give written notification to landlord explaining your intention to vacate. (This may need to be done sooner than 6 weeks before leaving, or possibly later in the process.) Whatever your situation may be, giving "proper notification" is essential. Don't overlook this step.

- Arrange to have school records transferred. Obtain copies of college transcripts.

- Use a video camera to inventory contents of each room. Take close-up pictures of antiques and other valuables.

- Accumulate important and/or valuable documents that will be traveling with you.

- Obtain estimates for transporting boxes using alternate methods.

- Obtain prices for travel plans (hotel, airlines, etc.).

- Start collecting a variety of sturdy boxes and newspaper.

- Discuss the transfer of your homeowner's policy and other insurance needs with your insurance agent. If you are transporting "valuables", find out how to get the proper coverage for them.

- Try to obtain a floor plan and room measurements of the new residence.

- Notify all professional people of your intention to relocate (doctor, dentist, pharmacist, banker, veterinarian, lawyer, stockbroker, etc.). Make sure all records are complete and ready to be sent upon request. Ask each one for referrals in your new community.

- Notify banking institutions. Find out what needs to be done when transferring funds to a bank in another state. If possible, establish an account with a bank in the new community. Otherwise, you may have a problem trying to cash checks from an out-of-state account.

- Close local charge accounts with community businesses. However, retain major credit cards until you have an opportunity to obtain new ones through local banks at destination.

- Obtain information about your destination city through the Chamber of Commerce, real estate agent, etc.

- Deliver rugs to the dry cleaners.

- Discuss the upcoming relocation with all family members (especially children). Make each member a part of the planning process. Surprises will only contribute to a traumatic experience. Explain all of the advantages.

- Return borrowed items and collect things loaned to others.

- If your employer is paying for the move, find out exactly what they will pay for. Don't leave anything in doubt.

- If you still need to sell your house, escalate your efforts. If you are working with a real estate company, make sure it is properly advertising the property.

- If you are planning a house-hunting trip, start making arrangements. Try to obtain the Sunday edition of the local newspaper at destination. It will have a large real estate section to guide you. (Once you find a new residence measure openings for placement of all appliances.)

- Obtain change-of-address cards from the Post Office, and compile a list of those who need to receive one. (Once you have secured a new residence, notify the P.O. and send out cards.)

- Start consuming frozen foods and canned goods.

- If antiques, valuable items and/or collectibles need to be moved, consider obtaining an expert appraisal of each item. In addition, take pictures for verification.

- Obtain IRS "Moving Expense" form. (Your local library or P.O. may have one in stock.)

- Do repair work and painting.

FOUR WEEKS BEFORE:

- Select the moving company which offers the best services, at the most reasonable price (even if an exact schedule for loading/delivery is not known yet).

- Begin packing items that are seldom used.

- If your shipment needs to be placed in a self-storage facility at destination, start working on a location through friends, relatives, fellow workers, etc.

- If pets need to be transported, make special arrangements. Get immunization shots and documentation papers from the veterinarian.

- If you are applying for membership to new clubs, apply now if you anticipate a waiting list.

- Inform Federal and State tax agencies, and the State Motor Vehicle Dept. of necessary changes.

TWO WEEKS BEFORE :

- Confirm all travel arrangements.

- If traveling by automobile, have it serviced and totally prepared for the trip.

- If elevator usage is needed, reserve it through the apartment manager.

- Arrange to have grandfather clock/pool table disassembled by an expert. Call the store where they were purchased to get recommendations.

- Notify all utility companies of the exact shut-off date at origin, and the turn-on date at destination (telephone, gas, electric, water).

- Notify other service companies (newspaper, gardener, diaper service, etc.).

- Increase efforts to collect and/or purchase boxes and continue the packing process.

- Ask your employer/manager for a generalized "letter of recommendation". Even though it may not be needed immediately, it's nice to have a year or two later.

- Mail all remaining change-of-address cards.
  (This is assuming you have a new address at this time.)

- Make sure all tax assessments are paid.

- Call the representative from the moving company selected, to review details and confirm scheduling. If you have added or deleted items, let the representative know. If you want to add extra services or delete a service already added into the total cost, now is the time to update changes. It may be necessary to complete an "addendum" reflecting these changes.

- Start "bidding farewell" to friends and relatives. Make a few phone calls each day. Otherwise, you will be bombarded with calls and personal visits during your last few days. Trying to accomplish last-minute chores will become impossible.

- Call friends, neighbors, and relatives to pick up items you intend to give away.

- Conduct a second garage sale, if the first one was not successful.

- Call a charitable organization to make a contribution. (Keep receipt for a possible federal tax deduction.)

ONE WEEK BEFORE :

- Make sure the moving company has all the information necessary to communicate and deliver your shipment (address, telephone number at new residence, at new place of employment, at hotels, motels, at neighbors, friends, relatives, etc.).

- If traveling by car, pack emergency tool box to be kept in trunk.

- Begin packing all suitcases.

- Pack the "Car-Box", the "Quick-Fix" Box, and the "Keep With You At All Times Suitcase".

- Dispose of remaining flammables, aerosol cans, explosives, matches, etc.

- Accumulate all documents/important papers and valuables that are traveling with you.

- Make final arrangements to close and/or transfer bank accounts and safety deposit box. Buy travelers checks and obtain a cashier's check or certified check to pay the moving company.

- Drain fuel and oil from lawn mower, other motorized equipment, and power tools.

- Clean outdoor barbeque. Pack removable parts.
  (Make sure propane tank is empty.)

- Replace fixtures that will be going and finish minor repair work.

- If your employer is being billed by the moving company, make sure the "purchase order" or "letter of authority" has been received. Since the moving company will conduct a credit investigation, make sure your employer has received credit approval. This is very important! If it has not received something in writing from your company, and approved the company's credit, you will be expected to pay the driver when he arrives at the new residence.

- Arrange to have all major appliances serviced and prepared for the trip. (If you are disconnecting gas/water hook-ups, you can wait until a few days before moving.)

- Arrange for a baby-sitter on "pack-day" and/or moving day.

- If you are shipping boxes through the Post Office or using another alternative, make arrangements to deliver the boxes. Arrange the drop-off in conjunction with your travel plans. You may not want them to arrive too soon.

- If you are entitled to refunds and/or deposit money from utility companies, landlord, or club memberships, make sure they all have your new address. If possible, try to obtain your money while still living there. It beats long-distance telephone calls and letter writing.

- If any legal matters are unresolved, call your attorney to discuss details.

- Start packing pictures, paintings, mirrors, and other wall decorations.

- Sell, donate, or give away remaining house plants.

- Consume food items that are not going with you. Sell or give away what remains.

- Complete all laundry chores.

- Have a "farewell party" for neighbors, friends, and relatives. Keep it simple, and consider using an abundance of paper and plastic products.

- Remove breakables, bottles and jewelry from all drawers. Fill spaces with towels, etc.

ONE-TWO DAYS BEFORE :

- If you are doing your own packing, everything should be ready (except for a few boxes of necessities that can be done on moving day, before the truck arrives).

- Have professional packers arrive to pack the items agreed upon beforehand. (If only a few boxes need to be packed, they are usually done on moving day.)

- Discard items in drawers and cupboards that are not going.

- If residence will be vacant, notify police and neighbors.

- Check steam iron to make sure all water has been drained.

- If you will be paying according to the "actual weight" of your load and have informed the company of your intent to "witness the weighing procedure", call the company to remind them.

- Call and remind baby sitter of schedule. Arrange to have pets out of the way.

- Finish labeling items and/or boxes that state "Do Not Load", "Load Last", "Fragile", "This Side Up", etc.

- Start the cleaning process.

- Prepare a local map for the driver to use to find your new residence.

- Retrieve clothing/rugs from the dry cleaners.

- Disassemble large furniture pieces.

- Confirm airline and hotel/motel reservations.

- Begin packing the car.

- Remind all utility companies, newspaper, and other service companies of shut-off day.

- Put your new address on a small piece of paper and tape it to the side of a kitchen cupboard. The new occupants will need to forward mail that is inadvertently sent to the old address.

- Empty and disconnect major appliances (stove, refrigerator, washer, dryer, window air conditioner, etc.). Plan on going out to dinner on the night before moving day and also on moving day. (Have you collected all appliance manuals for the new owners?)

- Empty, defrost, and clean the refrigerator/freezer and allow to thoroughly dry. Keep checking the drainage tray under the appliance and remove the water. Place baking soda in each compartment.

- Arrange taxi service to the airport. (If you are going in a friend's vehicle, confirm the schedule to arrive in ample time.)

MOVING DAY:

- Finish packing the car.

- Isolate all boxes and suitcases that are traveling with you.

- Disassemble the waterbed.

- Stay calm and let the movers do their job. Be available to answer questions.

- Review all details on the "Bill of Lading". Make sure everything, especially the "valuation coverage", is filled in correctly before signing.

- Review all details for delivery. Verify addresses, phone numbers, scheduling, etc.

- Accompany the movers when the inventory is taken. Check their notations and make your own, if necessary. Make sure everything receives an inventory number. Then, sign all inventory sheets and retain a copy.

- Place soft drinks, cold cuts, etc. in a cooler that can be used during the day.

- Remove pillows and blankets from beds.
  (Leave the mattress/boxspring covers intact.)

- Place trash bags at the curb. If your trash day is not until a few days later, ask neighbors about using their trash cans. It's better than having dogs rip open plastic bags, spreading the contents throughout the neighborhood.

- Vacuum and/or sweep room as it is emptied.

- Check all drawers/closets for remaining items that could have been overlooked. (Have you emptied your secret hiding places?)

- Return keys to new owners, apartment manager, realtor, lawyer, etc.

- Do not use your television sets. Experts say that they should be at room temperature when taken out of a residence. (If they are too hot, cracking may occur.)

- If you notice any damage caused by the movers, make notations on your copy of the inventory and the driver's copy.

- Have cash available to provide a tip for the movers.

- Check all windows and doors to be sure they are locked.

AT DESTINATION :

- Contact the local agent for the moving company to inform the agent of any change in delivery address, telephone numbers, etc.

- Inform the local Post Office of which day you actually plan on moving in. (See if any mail has already been forwarded.)

- Arrange to have all utilities turned on. Find out about deposits needed.

- Check plumbing/heating system, electrical outlets, built-in appliances, smoke detectors, etc.

- Do minor repair work, painting and wallpapering. (It is easier when rooms are still empty.)

- Clean entire house. Line cupboards with shelving paper.

- Introduce yourself to neighbors and ask about local stores to buy food, hardware, and other services.

- Have duplicate keys made immediately.

- Arrange for newspaper delivery.

- Register children in the new school system.

- Contact local banks and establish new accounts.

- Contact insurance agent for your immediate needs. (home, automobile, health)

- Contact Department of Motor Vehicles, Voter Registration, and the pet licensing authority.

- Make arrangements to have major appliances reconnected if you are not doing it yourself.

- Check the placement of telephone outlets and arrange to lease or buy new phones, if needed.

- Make arrangements with a long-distance telephone service company. (Shop around!!) You will probably have an immediate need for long-distance communication.

- Decide on the proper placement of furniture. Discuss which child gets the larger bedroom.

MOVE-IN DAY:

- Pay the driver, unless other arrangements have been prearranged.

- Check-off numbers on inventory sheets. One person should be outdoors, while a second person is indoors, directing the movers to the proper room locations. Inspect furniture and boxes for possible damage. If any damage is observed or a box is crushed and/or dented, make notations on your copy and the driver's copy of the inventory sheet. Open boxes that appear damaged to inspect the contents while the driver is still there to observe any damage.

- Allow all appliances and televisions a chance to warm up to room temperature before using. This is very important if the outdoor temperature is extremely cold.

- If a battery-operated radio is available, tune into a station that plays relaxing music.

- If you are paying to have the movers do some of the unpacking, supervise this procedure after everything has been positioned in its proper place.

- Do not get involved in trying to unpack everything yourself during the unloading. This can be done in the days that follow.

- Have cash available to tip the movers.

- Arrange to have dinner at a nice restaurant. (Reward yourselves!)

NOTES:

SECTION 12

HELPFUL ORGANIZATIONAL TIPS

"Do not be afraid to ask questions of each moving company. You may get answers that will help you avoid hassles, save time, and maybe even save money". -The author

---

1. When is a good time to begin the packing process?

   Start packing infrequently used items, *one month in advance*. Slowly whittle away at this time-consuming chore, a few boxes at a time. Don't underestimate the amount of boxes needed to pack. When purchasing or collecting boxes, make sure you have an ample supply of various sizes. It's better to have a few left over, than to frantically dash around at the last minute when your time is limited.

2. Does it make any difference if I pack similar items from various rooms, in the same box?

   Try to pack room-by-room. It will save a bundle of time when unpacking takes place.

3. What can be done to minimize the liklihood of a box getting crushed?

   Always place wadded-up paper slightly above the top of a box. Then, apply a little pressure before taping the flaps down. Apply tape to the middle seam, and to both edges. Since some of the boxes may be placed on their side, you don't want the

Apply tape to the middle seam, and to both edges. Since some of the boxes may be placed on their side, you don't want the contents to be able to move if that should happen. In theory, pretend you are sitting on a suitcase to squeeze it shut! But, never overpack a box so that it has bulges.

4. Is there anything different about the packing paper used by the professionals, and regular newspaper?
The consistency is about the same. The main difference is that packing paper has no news on it (ink). Never let newspaper come in direct contact with items that can be soiled by the ink. It is fine to use, but you must take a few precautions. First, use tissue paper or plastic baggies, then wrap in newspaper. In addition, constantly wash your hands to remove the ink.

5. Are there any weight limitations for a box?
Never pack boxes so they get too heavy. Keep each box under 50 pounds, since packing tape will only hold so much weight. The last thing you want to see is the bottom falling out of a box.

6. What items should go into a box first?
Place the heaviest things at the bottom. Save the upper area for the lighter and more delicate items.

7. Can pots and pans, silverware and other kitchen items be placed into the same boxes with kitchen dishes, glasses, etc.?
Never pack fragile items in the same box with other categories. Keep them separated to avoid potential damage.

8. Why is it necessary to make notations on the side of a box?
Once boxes are stacked on top of each other, you can't read the notes written on the top. Plus, when everything is unloaded at destination, boxes may be stacked in a room or garage area. They can be easily organized to avoid sore back muscles as a result of moving them around in order to read the notes written on the top.

9. What about packing the prized moosehead and the antique crystal chandelier?
For large, delicate, or odd-shaped items, a wooden crate

should be specially constructed. If it's worth moving, it's worth packing properly.

10. Do small furniture items have to be packed into boxes?

If something will conveniently fit in a box, put it in one. Take the time to disassemble little tables, floor lamps, etc. Small foot stools and plant stands should go into boxes. The more uniformity your shipment has, the tighter everything will pack inside the truck. That means less chance for movement and/or shifting of the shipment.

11. Can I pack my small kitchen appliances into the same boxes they came in?

If the original box and packing material is available, use it. Then, consolidate by placing these small boxes into larger sturdy containers.

12. What should I do with the empty boxes, once the move is completed?

After unpacking, remove tape so the boxes can be easily folded and stored in a flat position. Place in a dry area of the attic or garage. Usually the open area of the cross-beams near the ceiling is ideal. Place plastic over them to keep clean for the next time. Don't be foolish enough to think there will not be a next time. "Never say, Never!"

13. Should a protective coating of wax be put on wooden furniture, just before loading on the truck?

This makes the furniture slippery and hard to handle. It also increases the likelihood of the furniture pads sliding off, due to road vibrations. Once you are settled in, polish everything.

14. How long should I wait before hanging pictures, paintings and mirrors on the walls?

It can take several weeks before you feel totally comfortable with the positioning of furniture in every room. Wait a few weeks before pounding nails into the walls. Unless there is absolutely no other wall where a particular item would look good, restrain yourself for awhile. Resist the immediate temptation to get "hammer happy".

15. Who should be notified that I'm moving? And, what is the easiest way to do it?

Free change-of-address cards can be picked up at any branch of the U.S.Post office. Here is a partial list of whom to notify:

- local Post Office
- friends/relatives
- magazine subscriptions
- banks
- credit card companies
- lawyer
- doctor/dentist/veterinarian/pharmacist
- Social Security Office/Internal Revenue Service
- church/synagogue
- former employer (to send tax form for wages earned)
- Department of Motor Vehicles

Do not forget to stop by the local Post Office at destination, immediately upon arrival. There may be mail waiting for you.

16. What needs to be checked on an automobile just prior to a long-distance trip?

Have your mechanic check the brakes and tires. If you are traveling during the winter months, snow tires should be a definite consideration. At the very least, a set of tire chains should be available. The antifreeze and coolant system need to be inspected. In general, a tune-up with a complete inspection ought to be performed. The last thing you need is to be stranded in "no man's land" for a few days!

17. Is there a convenient way to make hotel/motel reservations along the route we intend to be driving?

Visit the local branch of a large motel chain to obtain information regarding its national network. Many provide a directory which explains the services offered, prices, and locations. Most will accept major charge cards which provide an easy method of documenting your moving expenses.

18. Since we will arrive at destination before the truck, how can we cut down on motel expenses?

If you don't mind "roughing it" for a few days, consider the

174

use of sleeping bags and air mattresses. These purchases should be cheaper than lodging costs. In addition, instead of receiving a handshake at check-out time, you will still have these items for future use.

19. If we are able to occupy our present residence until the last day of the month, should we schedule the pickup on that day?

Whenever possible, try to schedule the pickup for a few days prior to the date you must legally be out of the residence. This allows some flexibility in case the truck is delayed. Sometimes the driver can be late due to circumstances that are beyond his control (bad weather, mechanical problems, etc.). You don't want the new occupants moving in on the day you are moving out. Try to avoid this potentially hostile encounter!

20. Will the movers remove items in the rafters of a garage/attic, or in a "crawl-space"?

Only if they feel it is safe, *and* only if they get paid an extra hourly labor charge to do so. They are not obligated to climb ladders; walk across dangerous flooring; walk into areas where they are unable to stand erect; or go into any area that is not adequately lighted.

21. In this deregulated industry, how can I find out exactly the services, rules and regulations of each company?

Ask questions of each company representative. Some companies have "exceptions" filed with the I.C.C. In other words, a company may want to charge a different price, or provide a different service than what is presently offered by other companies.

22. How can I be sure the quality of service will be excellent if companies are discounting?

Only the creative companies that continue to provide the best service, and adjust their philosophy, will survive and flourish. So far, the quality of service provided by the major companies has remained constant, irregardless of discounts. It is still too early to tell how discounted prices will effect the quality of service in the future. While companies may be receiving less revenue for each move, they should be transporting more volume. With a lower price, the gap between using a professional company and a do-it-yourself move is smaller.

175

23. If my employer is paying for the move, *and has a separate contract with the moving company,* are the same set of rules, regulations, and prices applied?

While interstate moving companies must comply with all I.C.C. requirements, a contract between the moving company and your employer may contain certain conditions or limitations that are perfectly acceptable to the I.C.C. This is especially true with government/military relocations. You should ask your employer and the representative from the moving company about any provisions, exceptions, conditions, or limitations contained in a separate contractual agreement between them.

24. What type of items should I instruct the driver to load last on the van?

It is your responsibility to inform the movers of any items or boxes that you would like to be loaded last. In doing so, they will be the very first things to be unloaded at destination. Typical items would include the vacuum cleaner, rugs and pads, a few boxes containing kitchen supplies or toys for the children.

25. Should I be present when my shipment is weighed?

If you received a non-binding estimate based on the actual weight of your household, it is a good idea to be present at *both weigh-ins.* The truck will drive over a certified scale before arriving on moving day. After the entire shipment is loaded, the driver will return to a scale for a second weigh-in. You will be obligated to pay for the weight difference between those two figures. You have the right to witness both procedures. However, you must inform the company before moving day, so it can properly notify you of the time and place to meet. If you decide to witness the weigh-ins, make sure you are present *both times.*

26. What are common misconceptions concerning free services provided by a professional mover?

Some people expect the movers to disconnect lighting fixtures and appliances, and reconnect everything at destination. Also, some people are shocked to discover that boxes and packing materials are not free.

27. What needs to be done inside the new residence, before the truck arrives?

Scour the entire house using an ample supply of "elbow grease". If you do not know where to purchase some, you are in big trouble! All shelves can be lined with paper. Start the painting and wallpapering process in the rooms which will contain the most furniture. It will be easier and faster to complete while they are empty. Also, discuss the proper placement for large pieces of furniture; make arrangements with all utility companies; arrange for appliance hookups, if needed; and inspect plumbing/heating systems.

"Dearest, when does the fun, excitement and adventure begin?"

SECTION 13

THE DO-IT-YOURSELF INTERSTATE MOVE

"Daddy, is it worth it? I'd be willing to go without candy and gum for a whole year."
  - Phillip, Jr., 4 years old, to parents Phil and Elaine, in need of a restroom after the first five miles.

Interstate truck rental companies have continued to increase their rates over the past few years (since deregulation of the professionals). Even though the professionals have also raised their rates, discounting brings them closer to what they were charging at the beginning of the 1980's. This is good news for the consumer, but not welcomed news for the professional moving companies.

The most common reason for not using a professional company is cost. Those who undertake the "adventure" of a self-move are usually trying to save money. If you are among the young and/or adventurous-at-heart who are contemplating a do-it-yourself relocation, the following information can be used to estimate the costs involved. When you finish adding up all of the little "extras", you may decide that the money saved is simply not worth the hassle. Do not "bury your head in the sand" while underestimating the total cost. Being unrealistic will only result in financial problems "down the road".

Since your relocation will probably be many miles away, it is doubtful that borrowing a friend's truck will be a possibility. Therefore, you will need to start shopping at truck rental locations to find the best price for a van and any other necessary equipment. Since these companies are as competitive as the professional moving companies, expect the rental rates to vary. In addition, you can expect a variance depending on the size of the truck, the season (higher during the summer months), and the city of origin and destination.

Visit a few of the major truck rental companies in your area. They provide free booklets which explain the equipment available. In addition, the brochures offer advice on how to anticipate what you will need to accomplish this task. (Estimating the proper truck size, packing and loading tips, etc.)

It is extremely important to obtain an accurate estimate for the proper-sized truck. It is common for non-professionals to underestimate the amount of space needed to accommodate a shipment of household goods. There is always "wasted space" due to odd-shaped pieces of furniture. The professional movers are experts at making "every inch count". It is doubtful that you could fit as much into the same amount of space.

The booklets offered by truck rental companies can be helpful in estimating "cubic capacity". In addition, when the representatives from professional moving companies tour your home, they will estimate the total cubic footage needed on their trucks. Since you do not want to leave a bedroom set on the front lawn, get the rental price for a truck that can hold a larger capacity. It's better to be safe, than sorry!

Before you obtain truck rental estimates, a major consideration must be explained. Some of the smaller-sized trucks can be rented with automatic transmissions (11-15 foot vans). A 15 foot truck is only capable of transporting approximately 3 average rooms full of household goods. If you have that many rooms, along with some major appliances or an abundance of items in a garage, attic or basement, there is a good chance you will need a larger-sized truck. If this is the case, you and your traveling companion should be prepared to drive a "stick-shift"! While some companies do have a few of the larger-sized vans equiped with automatic transmissions, they are not readily available.

Use the following outline to arrive at a realistic price. Compare this total estimated cost with those from the professional companies. Then, read the important considerations which follow. Whatever your ultimate decision may be, make it an educated one!

Truck Rental .... _____

Redistribution Fee .... _____

Handcart (with and/or without straps) .... _____

Dolly (platform on four wheels)........................ _____

Insurance Coverage(for truck damage/accident liability, etc.) _____

Furniture Pads @ $____per doz. for ____dozen = _____

Straps/Ropes (to secure shipment inside the truck) _____

Boxes and Materials...................................... _____

Tolls/Bridges (higher for trucks) .... _____

Permits .... _____

Tow Bar Rental (for car)................................. _____

Loading Labor (friends?)............................... _____

State Sales Tax (find out what will be taxed).......... _____

Sub-Total _____

Once you arrive at a sub-total that realistically estimates the cost of all "extras" needed, the cost to purchase gasoline is next. Most rental trucks will get approximately 5-7 miles to a gallon.

Total Miles _____ ÷ 5 miles per gallon = _____ gallons

_____ gallons X $_____ for each gallon = $_____ Total

(When calculating the cost of each gallon, figure high since the main highways will not have cheap "self-service"gas stations for your convenience.)

Add the total estimated cost for gasoline to the sub-total. Now, you are ready to estimate the additional cost for motels and food. When estimating motel costs, be realistic about prices you can expect along the main highways. These rooms are not cheap. In addition, if you need more than one bed, be expecting to pay a higher rate.

Motel cost per night $_____ X _____ nights = $_____ Total

Food cost per meal $_____ X _____ meals per day = $_____ Total

$_____ per person X _____ people = $_____ Total per day

$_____ total per day X _____ days = $_____ Total food cost

(When calculating motel and food, you should take into account any extra time needed on the road, since it may take longer than by automobile.)

SUB-TOTAL $_____

GASOLINE $_____

MOTEL $_____

FOOD $_____

TOTAL ESTIMATED COST $_____

"I didn't say it would be *easier*, sweetcheeks!"

IMPORTANT CONSIDERATIONS

Now that you realize the amount of money needed to perform the move yourself, compare this price to that of the professionals. If you plan on driving your automobile, you may want to make adjustments to account for expenses that you will have anyway (motel, food, and gasoline for car).

The convenience and safety offered by the professionals is often worth the extra amount. But before making a decision based strictly on dollars and cents, give some thought to a few other important considerations.

• Are you and others who will be helping with loading and unloading, physically able to lift the heavy items without risking injury? Back and arm muscles which are not regularly used, will certainly be needed.

• Do you have dependable people at both origin and destination who can definitely be relied upon to show up?

• If you need to hire a person to assist at either end, did you calculate that cost into your total estimate?

• Did you estimate the correct number of furniture pads that need to be rented? Since these are about one-half the size of those used by professionals, you will need to rent almost twice as many. Most items (excluding boxes) will require at least one pad. Therefore, include enough in your estimate. You do not want to be skimpy with padding. This protection will help reduce the liklihood of seeing knicks, scratches and wood chips when unloading.

• What kind of insurance can be purchased in case an accident should occur? Is liability coverage available for injuries, as well as damage to the truck and/or contents?

• What kind of deposit is required on the vehicle? Most companies require a credit card or a large cash deposit.

• Does the rental company guarantee that you will get the truck you need, on the exact day you need it? Will it be the right size, and have all the features you were promised (automatic transmission, radio, air conditioning)? If the company will not provide a written guarantee stating that the truck requested will be available on the day needed, be prepared for the possibility of a delayed departure. While this is not an everyday occurrence, it does happen!

• If you have mechanical problems, who do you contact for repairs or replacement of the truck?

• If the truck breaks down on a highway during the evening hours, what can you do when stranded? If this does happen, will the rental company pay for motel/food expenses, in addition to all necessary repair bills? Will you be expected to pay all of these bills "out of your own pocket", then wait to be reimbursed in the future? Will the company pay the labor cost for reloading the shipment on another truck, if this becomes necessary?

• What is the additional cost for each day you must keep the truck, past the total number of days allowed for your trip? This is especially important for those who must secure a residence at destination. One may not be readily available. Sometimes, you are required to wait until the first day of the following month.

• If your belongings need to be placed in a storage facility at destination, how much will it cost to continue renting the furniture pads? You will still need protection for some of the items being placed on top of each other while being stored.

NOTES:

COMMENTS ??

The publisher and author are extremely interested in hearing from you. (Both good news and/or bad news!)

This information will enable us to help others in the future, and will be incorporated in the next edition of this book.

Comments (attach separate sheet, if necessary):

Name: _____

Address:_____

City: _____ State: _____ Zip:_____

Telephone (optional): _____

Please send comments to the address below, and let us know if we have permission to use your comments in the future.

_____ Yes, you may use my name when quoting from my comments.

Signature: _____

TRANSPORTATION PUBLISHING CO.
P.O.Box 2309-B
Mission Viejo, CA 92690

ORDER FORM

Transportation Publishing Co.
P.O. Box 2309-B
Mission Viejo, CA 92690

      Please send me _____ copies of Moving? Don't Be Taken For An Expensive Ride at $12.95 each, plus $1.50 per copy to cover shipping costs for each book.

Name: _____

Address: _____

City: _____ State: _____ Zip: _____

* For shipments within California add 6% sales tax per book ($.80).

____ I cannot wait 3-4 weeks for book rate shipping. I am enclosing $3.00 per book for Air Mail Delivery.

---

* Would you like to order this book as a special gift for a friend, neighbor or relative anticipating an interstate relocation? Please indicate the complete name and address of person(s) to receive a copy.

Name: _____

Address: _____

City: _____ State: _____ Zip: _____

ORDER FORM

Transportation Publishing Co.
P.O. Box 2309-B
Mission Viejo, CA 92690

Please send me ____ copies of Moving? Don't Be Taken
For An Expensive Ride at $12.95 each, plus $1.50 per copy to
cover shipping costs for each book.

Name: _____

Address: _____

City: _____ State: _____ Zip: _____

* For shipments within California add 6% sales tax per book
($.80).

____ I cannot wait 3-4 weeks for book rate shipping. I am
enclosing $3.00 per book for Air Mail Delivery.

* Would you like to order this book as a special gift for a friend,
neighbor or relative anticipating an interstate relocation? Please
indicate the complete name and address of person(s) to receive a
copy.

Name: _____

Address: _____

City: _____ State: _____ Zip: _____